W elcome to the premier edition of Fishing B.C. This book covers the Thompson/Nicola Region of beautiful British Columbia, Canada. This area is renowned for its' excellent fly fishing and large Kamloops Trout.

The Thompson/Nicola Region covers a large part of the interior of B.C. The hot dry climate, rolling hills and the abundance of small nutrient rich lakes makes this area a fisherman's paradise. The trout grow quickly and are readily taken on a fly. The lakes also offer several other fish species which helps provide the versatility and challenge many anglers crave.

In this book we have provided depth charts of over 100 of the best fishing lakes in the region. To ensure you have a successful trip, we have also provided information on access, facilities, fishing hints, fly hatches, stocking and surrounding lakes. The lakes in our book range from easily accessible lakes with resorts to remote hike-in only lakes. Further, we have added a good variety of higher elevation and deeper lakes that offer good fishing throughout the ice-free season. Where possible, we have also included information on ice fishing.

Since a lot of the lakes in the Thompson/Nicola Region require you to weave your way through a maze of logging roads, we recommend you pick up a copy of the Backroad Mapbook for the Kamloops/ Okanagan area. This book has very detailed maps along with descriptions on everything from camping areas to fishing lakes. It is the perfect compliment to the Fishing B.C. book for the Thompson/Nicola Region.

No other source combines such detailed information on the best lakes in the Thompson/ Nicola Region. If you are new to the area or are looking for where to fish we are certain you will find Fishing B.C. an excellent guide.

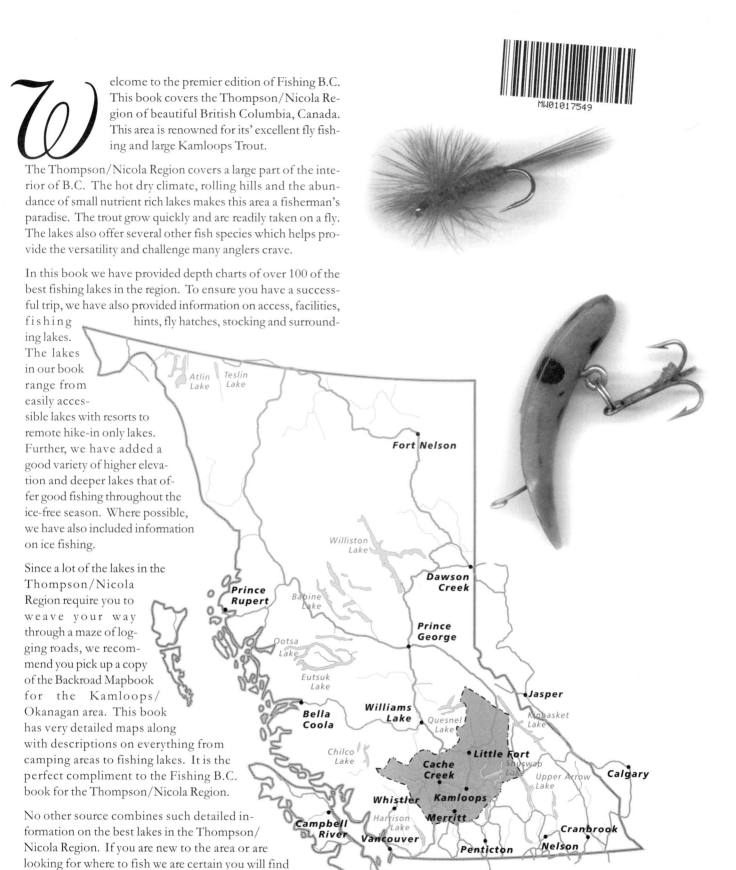

FISHING BC

DIRECTORS
Penny Mussio
Russell Mussio
Wesley Mussio

EDITOR IN CHIEF
Russell Mussio

ART DIRECTOR
Brandon Tam

PRODUCTION
Kelly Briggs
Trevor Daxon
Brett Firth
Brandon Tam
Dale Tober

WRITERS
Wesley Mussio
Russell Mussio

CANADIAN CATALOGUING IN PUBLICATION DATA

Mussio, Wesley, 1964-

Mussio Ventures Ltd. presents Fishing BC:
British Columbia's Best Fishing Lakes.

Written by Wesley and Russell Mussio.
Includes indexes.
Contents: v. 1. Thompson-Nicola.
ISBN 0-9685611-0-1 (v. 1)

1. Fishing–British Columbia–Guidebooks. 2. British Columbia–Guidebooks. I. Mussio, Russell, 1969-. II. Title. III. Title: Fishing BC.

SH572.B8M88 2000   7995.19'09711   C99-901640-7

Published by:

232 Anthony Court
New Westminster, B.C. V3L 5T5
P. (604) 520-5670   F. (604) 520-5630
E-mail: info@backroadmapbooks.com
www.backroadmapbooks.com
Copyright © 2000 Mussio Ventures Ltd.

Table of Contents

Thompson/Nicola Lakes

The Thompson/Nicola Region attracts over 50% of all of British Columbia's Freshwater Fishing enthusiasts. Not only can you fish a lake a day, but the fast growing trout are readily taken on flies, lures and spinners.

In this region, seasonal water temperatures usually determine the quality of fishing. Generally, after the ice melts in late April to early May, fish are feeding near the surface and are the easiest to catch. As summer approaches, the fish retreat to deeper waters to avoid the algae bloom and the warmer waters. At that time, the fishing success generally suffers and the summer doldrums are in full swing. By fall, the water temperatures drop again and the fish return to the surface. With fewer anglers, the fishing success definitely improves in the fall. By late November, ice can start forming. From December to April 30, many of the lakes are closed to protect the lakes from over fishing.

In most lower elevation lakes (less than 1200m or 4000 ft), fishing is best in late May to June and again in late September to October. Higher elevation lakes offer good fishing through the summer months as the water tends to stay cold enough to keep the trout actively fishing.

Fly fishing is the best fishing method in the Thompson/Nicola area given that the primary food source for the trout are aquatic insects and invertebrates. Use a fly corresponding with the hatch and you will have the best chance of success. The choice of the fly pattern not only depends on the hatch but also is based on the colour of the lake bottom and the type of vegetation in the lake.

If you are not able to match the hatch, use a sinking line with a Doc Spratley. This fly, fished deep, always seems to produce regardless of the lake. Shrimp and leech patterns can be productive all year round as there is not a set hatch for them.

Fly fishing near protection (eg. drop-off or logs), near food (eg. weeds, inflows or outflows) and in the thermocline (between the warm surface water and the cold water) produces the best results.

Gang trolls such as the Willow Leaf & worm or Ford Fender are the most effective trolling gear when trolling (see the Freshwater Fishing Regulations for bait bans). Lures, plugs and spinners are not that effective in the smaller lakes when trolling except when eastern brook trout are present. A leech pattern, bar none, is the most productive fly to troll around a lake, particularly in murky water. If trolling for eastern brook trout, try a Deadly Dicks with worm or a Flatfish.

Ice fishing is offered on a limited number of lakes (see the Freshwater Fishing Regulations for closures). Generally, the lakes containing brook trout offer the best results as brook trout are more active in the winter months. The fish generally are found at one level under the ice corresponding with the water level containing sufficient amounts of oxygen. Winterkill is a problem in the area.

Please Note: There are regulations imposed for many of the lakes in order to preseve the quality resource. Some of the regulations include bait bans, artifical fly only lakes, boating restrictions, catch & release and closures. Check the regulations before fishing!

Fly Fishing the Thompson/Nicola Lakes

The hatches in the Thompson/Nicola region are fairly predictable and a good fisherman can predict the hatch within a couple of days. Right at ice off, you should focus on dragonfly, leech and shrimp patterns. There is often a water boatman hatch as well. Shortly, the lake begins to turn over and fishing success is virtually non-existent for two weeks. This is because the oxygen deprived waters are being mixed with the oxygen rich waters making the available oxygen in the water dangerously low. The fish become extremely inactive and do not feed until the oxygen levels in the water increase.

As the oxygen levels increase and the waters warm, the chironomid (midge) hatch begins. On some lakes, the hatch can begin in late April and last until early June. Depending on the temperature, chironomid hatches may occur later.

Focusing on the chironomid hatch is becoming ever popular with the fly fishermen. The larvae (bloodworm), pupae and the adult stages of the hatch are all important food sources for the rainbow. Most fishermen use a pupa imitation with a floating line, long leader and a strike indicator. Sink the fly near the bottom in 20+ ft of water and retrieve it very slowly.

Beginning in late May and extending into early June, many of the lakes have a mayfly hatch. June sees the caddisfly (sedge) hatch. Fishermen should focus on dry flies as the adults caddis flies sit on the water surface drying their wings.

June produces some of the best dry fly fishing in the world. Cast a caddisfly in the morning and a mayfly in the evening.

July usually sees a good hatch of damselflies and in August, the dragonfly hatch is on.

By September, the chironomid hatch is back in full swing when the waters begin to cool. As the frost begins to appear in late September-early October, water boatman become more active. By October, leech, dragonfly and shrimp patterns are again the focus. Fishing a chironomid larvae (bloodworm) can be effective as well.

From ice-off to ice-on, the insects in the lakes of the region are shown in the Thompson/Nicola Hatch Chart above.

Thompson/Nicola Hatches

May:
- All chironomid stages
- Mayfly nymph
- Damselfly nymph
- Shrimp
- Leeches
- Dragonfly nymph

June:
- All chironomid stages
- Mayfly nymph
- Damselfly nymph
- Caddisfly/Sedge pupae
- Shrimp
- Leeches
- Dragonfly nymph

July:
- All chironomid stages
- Mayfly nymph
- Damselfly nymph
- Caddisfly/Sedge
- Shrimp
- Leeches
- Dragonfly nymph

August:
- All chironomid stages
- Mayfly nymph
- Damselfly nymph
- Caddisfly/Sedge
- Shrimp
- Leeches
- Dragonfly nymph

September:
- All chironomid stages
- Damselfly nymph
- Dragonfly nymph
- Shrimp
- Leeches
- Water boatman

October:
- Damselfly nymph
- Dragonfly nymph
- Shrimp
- Leeches

November:
- Shrimp
- Leeches
- Damselfly nymph
- Dragonfly nymph

Fish Species of the Thompson/Nicola Region

The common fish species found in the Thompson/Nicola Region are as follows:

Rainbow Trout are native to many streams and lakes in British Columbia. Due to their hardy nature and the fact they are an excellent sports fish, they are stocked throughout the province. Rainbow get their name from the colourful strip they get when spawning in the spring. The fish varies in size depending on the water body and strain you catch.

The Thompson/Nicola region is home to the world famous Kamloops Trout. This strain of rainbow grow very big, quickly. They offer a fantastic fight especially if caught on a fly. 4-5 lb (2 kg) Kamloops Trout are common but it is possible for these trout to grow over 9 kg (20 lbs). Fly fishing is very effective but spincasting with spoons and small spinners also works.

Eastern Brook Trout are actually char that were first introduced into B.C. in the early 1900's. The species is now found in many of the cooler streams and smaller mountain lakes in the province, where there is low concentration of oxygen that does not favor other species of trout. Brookies feed on insects and shrimp and are known to grow quickly in the Thompson/Nicola region. Easily identified by the large number of speckles, they are good fighters and very good tasting. Brook trout spawn in October and are known to be difficult to catch. They can be found to 2 lbs (1 kg) or larger.

Although any number of spinners and lures can be effective, spincasters should always try the most proven combination, a small Deadly Dick with a worm, cast from shore or from a boat towards shore. With the increase in popularity of fly fishing, you may hear many debates over what is the most effective way to catch this prized fish. Every lake seems to have its own preference. Depending on the time and season, the type of fly to use varies. During spawning season, large, attractor type flies can be very effective.

Kokanee are actually landlocked sockeye salmon that are stocked throughout the province. They are easily recognizable by their slim silver bodies with a forked tail. Kokanee turn a brilliant red and create an incredible display when they spawn in the late summer. In the plankton-rich interior lakes, they can reach 5 lbs (3 kg) but 10-12 inch (25-30 cm) fish are more common.

Kokanee are best caught on a Willow Leaf with a short leader and a Wedding Ring and maggot. Troll as slow as possible and in an "S" pattern so your line, will speed up or slow down and change depths as you round the bend. This entices the fish to bite. Troll-

ing with one ounce of weight or less, which takes the lure to 15 to 45 feet (5-14 m), is the most productive. It is possible to catch Kokanee on chironomids and Mayflies in the spring.

Dolly Varden & Bull Trout are the often confused species of the Char Family. They both have pinkish spots on the body but distinctly different heads. These fish spawn in the fall and are not known for their great fighting ability. The fish are found in larger lakes and a few streams in the Thompson/Nicola region. They prefer cold water and grow slowly. Dolly Varden can reach up to 20 lbs (9 kg) but 5-10 lb (2-5 kg) fish are more common. Their primary diet is insects, eggs and small fish.

In the larger lakes, an effective method of catching a dolly varden is to troll a green or orange Flat Fish or a Krocodile. Fishing the creek mouths with bait balls (a large cluster of worms and hook) can be deadly. Also, jigging with a bucktail and flasher in the winter or spring near a large creek mouth can be very successful. Due to significant declines in their population, tough regulations have been imposed in an effort to maintain the resource.

Lake Trout are only found in large, deep and cold lakes of the Thompson/Nicola region. They grow very slowly but often reaches sizes in excess of 25 lbs (10 kg) since they live longer than most other fish species. 5 lb (3 kg) fish are more common. Lake trout are not great fighters. This fall spawning fish is recognized by its forked tail, long head and large snout as well as an abundance of spots.

Since lake trout are predators any large shiny spoon, which imitates a minnow, is the lure of choice. These trout stay near the surface during the early spring and late fall when the water temperatures are cold. In the summer, the fish retreat to the depths of the lake so it is best to troll deep during summer months.

Whitefish are a silvery fish with large scales. They spawn in the fall and give a good fight even in the winter. They can reach 20 inches (50 cm) but average 12 inches (30 cm).

Whitefish are found in the larger Thompson/Nicola lakes but are not a popular sport fish due to the bony nature of their flesh. Similar to trout, they feed mainly on insects, although they are much more aggressive and less spooky than trout. Whitefish will readily strike spinners, spoons or shiny lures. They can be easily taken on a fly.

How to Read the Depth Charts

Knowing how to read a depth chart will definitely improve your fishing success. The reason being, the charts will show you where the fish are hanging out.

There are some good rules of thumb.

In small, clear water lakes, you should concentrate your efforts at the 3-10 m (10-25 ft) level. Review the depth charts and look for hidden islands, drop-offs and shoals. A hidden island is really a flat, shallow area surrounded by deeper water. A drop-off is identified as a rapid decline in depth on the chart. A shoal is a slowly declining area of the lake which then "drops off" into the depths. It is on the shoals where a fly fisherman should focus most of his/her efforts. This is because the shoals have most of the lake's aquatic vegetation and the insects and invertebrates upon which the fish feed live in the vegetation.

For larger lakes, the depth charts allow you to find the hidden ledges and drop-off areas. Try trolling along the drop-offs.

For small, dark water lakes, fish in shallower water (2-5 m or 5-15 ft) in the channels and near the weed beds.

Later in the evening before dusk, the rainbow begin to sneak ashore into the shallows to search for invertebrates and insects. Focus some of the casts into the shallows and you will be surprised with the results.

Creek estuaries are always a good bet as the fish congregate near the creek mouth in search of food. Bait and bobber are certain to produce. Be careful as the regulations may restrict you from using bait.

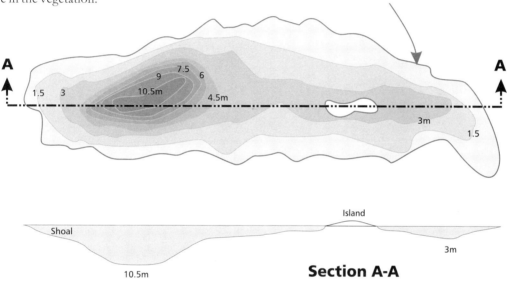

Section A-A

DEPTH CHART LEGEND

GEOGRAPHIC FEATURES & ROADS		MAP & RECREATION SYMBOLS		ABBREVIATIONS	
Flooded Land	Rocks	Anchorage	Hiking	CA	Catchables
Indian Reserves	Sandbars	Boat Launch	Lighthouse	FF	Fall Fry
Marshes	Shoals	Cabin / Resort	No Fishing	FR	Fry (similar to FF)
Provincial Parks	Swamp	Community	Parking	FG	Fingerlings
		Dam	Picnic Area	YE	Yearlings
Highways	Side Roads	Diving	Point of Interest	FSR	Forest Service Road
Main Roads	Other Roads	Float Plane Access	Truck Only Campground	ha	Hectare
		Highway, Primary	Trail or Water Access Campsite	ac	Acre
		Highway, Secondary	Trailer and Tent Campground	4wd	Four Wheel Drive Vehicles
		Highway, Trans-Canada	Waterfall	ft	Feet
				m	Meters
				kg	Kilogram
				lbs	Pounds

Allan Lake

Access/Parking

Allan Lake is one of the less scenic fishing lakes found in the Bonaparte Plateau. To reach the lake, head north from the Barrière turnoff on the Yellowhead Highway (Highway #5). Take a left at the Westsyde Road and then at the first major intersection, hang a right and you soon will be driving the Gorman Lake Road. After passing Gorman Lake, take a right at 17.5 km on the unmarked Scott Lake Forest Service Road and you will soon be at the east end of Allan Lake. The lake and rec site are found about 20 km form the highway. Bringing your RV to the lake isn't a wise idea but a 2wd truck is not a problem.

Fishing

Allan Lake is known as a whitefish hotspot. This agressive fish offers a good fishing experience throughout the year.

The lake is fairly deep (max. 15 m/50 ft) with a shallow, tree filled bay located to the east of the rec site. Since the bay averages less than 3 m (10 ft) deep in most of the water, there are few fish in the bay. It is best to fish the main body of the lake.

There are good shoals towards the southwest end of the main part of the lake. Also, the main part of the lake drops off nicely to its depths providing good shoals and nice drop-off where you should concentrate your fly fishing and spincasting efforts.

For fly fishermen, good hatches of insects such as mayflies, chironomids, damselflies and dragonflies are present. The water of the lake, given its high elevation and depth, remains fairly cool during the summer allowing the fishing to remain decent throughout the ice-free season. Expect a lot of company, as this lake is very popular especially during the summer months.

Trollers should stick to the center of the main part of lake and should try a gang troll, Flatfish or other small spinners.

Facilities

On the shallow tree filled bay, there is a forest service rec site. It has 15 camping units but only 4 tables along with a cartop boat launch and a dock. The unattractive rec site is heavily used especially during the summer months.

Other Options

The Bonaparte Plateau offers literally hundreds of lakes to sample:

Sandwiched between Allan Lake and Mayson Lake, the tiny **Bogmar Lake** offers rainbow to 1 kg (2 lbs). Be prepared to hike into the lake as the access road is very rough.

Other nearby options include **Bonaparte** and **Gorman Lakes**. These lakes are described in this book.

Lake Definition

Elevation:	1,183.5 m (3,883 ft)
Surface Area:	149.3 ha (368.9 ac)
Mean Depth:	6.7 m (22.1 ft)
Max Depth:	17.7 m (58 ft)
Perimeter:	10,076.8 m (33,960 ft)
Way Point:	51° 14' 00" Lat - N
	120° 21' 00" Lon - W

To Gorman Lake Rd

FSR

Lk

SCOTT

Allan Lake Rec Site

3 m
3
6
9
15
12 m
6
9
15
12 m
15 m
12
9
6 m
3

Thompson Nicola Region

Clearwater
Little Fort
Salmon Arm
Sicamous
Allan Lake
Cache Creek
Kamloops
Clinton
Lillooet
Merritt
Gold Bridge
Boston Bar
Spuzzum

Caverhill Lake
Darfield
5
GORMAN LAKE FSR
Allan Lake
JAMIESON Creek Rd
Bonaparte Lake
Akehurst Lake
Mayson Lake

N

Scale

200m 0 200m 400m 600m 800m 1000m

Alleyne Lake

Access/Parking

This 54.55 ha lake is found within the beautiful Kentucky-Alleyne Recreation Area southeast of Merritt. The recreation area is highlighted by open range land with encroaching forests. Several small lakes dot the landscape.

The lake is easily accessed off the Bates Road, a good 2wd road. It can either be reached by heading southwest from the Loon Lake interchange on the Okanagan Connector or by heading south on Highway 5 from the Aspen Grove Interchange and taking a left once you reach Bates Road.

Fishing

Alleyne Lake is a deep, clear lake (maximum 36 m/117 ft) highlighted by a sharp drop-off around most of its length. Even the small bay at the north end of the lake is 15 m (50 ft) deep. The lake receives heavy fishing pressure but it still produces well for rainbow to 2 kg (4-5 lbs) because of the plentiful shrimp and chironomid populations.

Given the depth of the lake, it is easily trolled using a gang troll or any number of lures such as a Blue Fox, Flatfish or Deadly Dick. Fly fishermen should focus their efforts at the drop-off and many marshy areas surrounding the lake.

Facilities

Alleyne Lake is located in the heart of the 144 ha Kentucky-Alleyne Recreation Area. The popularity of the recreation area is steadily increasing, but you are still likely to find a spot in the 63 vehicle/tent campsite throughout the summer months. The campground is rustic in nature as there are no showers, sani-station or flush toilets. Still, the surroundings are beautiful and the fishing is rewarding.

Other Options

Crater Lake is at 1000 m (3280 ft) in elevation and offers surprisingly good fishing for smaller rainbow that can reach 2 kg (5 lbs) in size. Trolling is the mainstay of the lake but fly fishermen should not be discouraged. The lake is 20 ha in size.

While at the recreation area, be sure to sample **Kentucky** or **Bluey Lake** to the south.

Lake Definition

Elevation:	976 m (3,200 ft)
Surface Area:	54.6 ha (135 ac)
Mean Depth:	16.8 m (55 ft)
Max Depth:	35.7 m (117 ft)
Perimeter:	4,667 m (15,312 ft)
Way Point:	49° 55' 00" Lat - N
	120° 34' 00" Lon - W

Recent Fish Stocking

Year	Fish Species	Life Stage	Number
1999	rainbow trout	YE	15,016
1998	rainbow trout	YE	10,000
1997	rainbow trout	YE	15,000
1996	rainbow trout	YE	14,902
1995	rainbow trout	YE	15,052

Scale

100m 0 100m 200m 300m 400m 500m

N

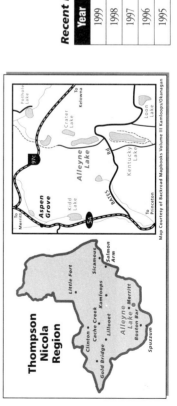

Map Courtesy of Backroad Mapbooks Volume III Kamloops/Okanagan

Thompson Nicola Region

Badger Lake

Access/Parking

The best access to this lake is actually found off of the Sun Peaks Road, found north of Kamloops on Hwy #5. Follow the Knouff Lake Road past both Knouff Lake and Little Knouff Lake before reaching Badger Lake. Badger Lake is about 23 km from the highway, the last few kilometers of which are muddy when wet. RV's and trailers can access the lake in dry weather only.

The more direct route would be along the Badger Lake FSR south of McClure. This road is not very well developed and rather confusing to follow. The road passes by a series of small lakes called the Struthers Lakes before reaching Badger Creek Forest Service Road and Badger Lake.

Facilities

There is nothing special about the rec site found next to the small lake. The scenery is okay and the large campsite is unshaded. There are 17 sites/picnic tables and a good boat launch. There is also a resort with camping nearby.

Fishing

Badger Lake is ideal for a vibrant fishery because it has dark, nutrient rich waters ideal for insect and plant life. In fact, Badger Lake use to produce trophy rainbow in the 5 kg (10 lb) range. However, heavy fishing has taken its toll and now the fish in the lake are substantially smaller but can reach 1.5 kg (3.5 lbs). To counteract the fishing pressure, a bait fishing and ice fishing ban was put in effect and the lake was stocked in 1990 with 4,000 rainbow, 1991 with 2,000 rainbow and 1994 with 2,500 rainbow. This management program has helped in improving the fishery over the last decade so now Badger Lake comes highly recommended. It is also sustained on a natural spawning program which should continue to work so long as the water remains high enough to allow active spawning.

For fly fishermen, the lake is best during the green sedge hatch in mid-June and the spring mayfly hatch. Early spring chironomid pupa fishing is fairly effective. Later in the spring and into the fall, try a caddisfly, leech or dragonfly pattern.

The lake is ice-free in early May until November. Focus your efforts around the island and try casting towards one of the many shoals that line the lake. Trolling a fly is a good bet.

Trolling the lake with gang trolls and lures is fairly difficult as the lake is shallow except in the area north of the island. Also, there are a lot of deadheads and debris in the lake that is certain to grab your gear.

Spincasters can work the shoreline casting a small green or silver Flatfish, Blue Fox, Deadly Dick or Frisky Fly near the fallen logs where the fish tend to hang out.

Luckily, the lake is not as susceptible to summer doldrums as other lakes in the area.

Other Options

If the fish are not biting at Badger Lake, try **Spooney Lake** which is separated from Badger Lake by a narrow channel at the west end of Badger Lake. This lake is 7 ha in size and has good insect hatches in the early spring. The rainbow grow to 1.5 kg (3.5 lbs) and tend to be larger than the Badger Lake fish. The same fishing methods for Badger Lake work for Spooney Lake.

Another option is **Little Badger Lake**, a 7 ha lake located to the northeast of Badger Lake along the Badger Creek FSR. The lake offers slow fishing for rainbows that can reach 1 kg in size. It is best to fly fish, bait fish or spincast the lake in the spring or fall.

Lake Definition

Elevation:	1,081 m (3,546 ft)
Surface Area:	56 ha (139 ac)
Mean Depth:	4.6 m (15 ft)
Max Depth:	15 m (48 ft)
Perimeter:	5,311 m (17,424 ft)
Way Point:	51° 02' 00" Lat - N
	120° 08' 00" Lon - W

Scale: 200m 0 200m 400m 600m

Thompson Nicola Region

Birch Lake Group

Access/Parking

The Birch Lake Group of lakes is comprised of Birch Lake, Phinetta Lake and Tortoise Lake.

To reach the chain of lakes, take Highway #24 north of Little Fort. Turn south on the western end of the Eakin Creek Road (the old Highway 24). If you reach Lac des Roches on Highway #24, you have gone past the Birch Lake Group. The old highway brings you right by the northern shores of Phinetta Lake. A side road before Phinetta Lake brings you south to Birch Lake.

Lake Definition (Birch Lake)

Elevation:	1,112.5 m (3651 ft)
Surface Area:	239.99 ha (59.5 ac)
Mean Depth:	20.12 m (66.3 ft)
Max Depth:	38.41 m (124 ft)
Perimeter:	7,894.42 m (25,892 ft)
Way Point:	51° 27' 00" Lat - N
	120° 30' 00" Lon - W

Lake Definition (Phinetta Lake)

Elevation:	1,112.5 m (3651 ft)
Surface Area:	27.52 ha (68 ac)
Mean Depth:	4.39 m (14.4 ft)
Max Depth:	16.15 m (53 ft)
Perimeter:	3,840.5 m (12,599.9 ft)
Way Point:	51° 28' 00" Lat - N
	120° 30' 00" Lon - W

Fishing

Birch Lake is a relatively deep (maximum 39 m/125 ft) and given its depth and elevation (1113 m /3650 ft), offers decent fishing throughout the summer months. Fishing is still the best during the spring or late fall.

The lake holds good numbers of rainbow which grow to 2+ kg (5 lbs) but are usually in the 0.5-0.75 kg (1-2 lbs) range. Trolling is by far the most popular method of fishing although fly fishermen certainly should not be discouraged because there are some nice shoals particularly at the east and the west ends of the lake. Trolling lures (Flatfish, Deadly Dick or Krocodile), flies (leech, dragonfly, Doc Spratley, muddler minnow) or gang trolls (Willow leaf or Ford Fender) is your best options. Please note there is an engine power restriction (no motors over 10 hp).

For fly fishermen wishing to cast a line, chironomid pupa, mayfly nymph, damselfly nymph, sedge and leech patterns are the focus so long as you match the hatch.

There is also a fishery for ling cod (burbot). Jigging in the depths of the lake is the best method of catching cod.

Phinetta Lake is the smallest lake in the Birch Lake Group. It only has a small 15 m (50 ft) deep hole so it is hard to troll. The lake has many shoals ideal for insect growth so it is a good fly fishing lake. The lake is also stocked with up to 15,000 rainbow every odd year.

Like Birch Lake, chironomid pupa, mayfly nymph, damselfly nymph, sedge and leech patterns are the flies of choice so long as you match the hatch. Spincasters should throw a small spoon or spinner towards the shallows.

Tortoise Lake is found south of Birch Lake and can be accessed by trail. The shallow lake has numerous bays and shoals to sample.

Recent Fish Stocking (Birch Lake)

Year	Fish Species	Life Stage	Number
1997	rainbow trout	FG	10,000
1996	rainbow trout	FF	9,642
1995	rainbow trout	FF	22,500

Facilities

Birch Lake has a cartop boat launch facility as well as a resort.

Phinetta Lake offers a convenient 3 site recreation site. The close proximity to Highway 24 allows RV's and trailers into the site.

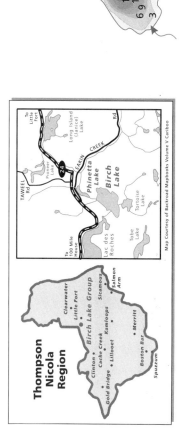

Bleeker Lake and No. 3 Lake

Access/Parking

Bleeker Lake is found north of the Roche Lake Provincial Park and to the east of the Kamloops-Merritt Highway (Highway #5A). Simply take the Roche Lake Road turnoff from Highway #5A. When you reach the provincial park, the Bleeker Lake Road takes off to the north soon reaching the southern shore of the lake. A 4wd vehicle is certainly the vehicle of choice as the Bleeker Lake Road is rough in places.

Fishing

Bleeker Lake is a 40 ha lake located at 1044 m (3425 ft) in elevation. The murky, nutrient-rich waters allow rainbow to grow to 3+ kg (7 lbs) so long as the lake is not exposed to winterkill, a problem in cold, long winters. That problem has recently been counteracted by an aerator, which is working but makes ice fishing treacherous because of thin ice.

The east end of the lake is quite shallow (less than 6 m) and there is a deep hole in the middle of the lake (12 m /40 ft deep). Because of this, the lake is covered with thick aquatic vegetation around its entire shores and fishing is restricted to the middle of the lake. Thus, you will need a float tube or boat to fish the lake.

Due to the shallow nature of the lake, it is best to use a floating line while fly fishing to keep your fly away from the weeds. Patterns of choice are a shrimp, leech or dragonfly. Trolling and spincasting are virtually impossible.

Your best bet is to fish the lake in the early spring before the weeds begin to choke the lake. In the summertime, the water warms, aquatic vegetation is rapidly growing and there is significant drawdown for irrigation purposes. This makes fishing virtually hopeless. It is not until the fall that fishing begins to pickup and you might be able to catch a larger fish.

Facilities

Facilities at the lake are quite limited but hand launching small boats is possible. Camping and good fishing can be found at the Roche Lake Group to the south.

Lake Definition (Bleeker Lake)

Elevation: 1,044 m (3,425 ft)
Surface Area: 38 ha (94 ac)
Mean Depth: 7.4 m (24.3 ft)
Max Depth: 13.7 m (44.9 ft)
Perimeter: 3,993 m (13,100 ft)
Way Point: 50° 30' 00" Lat - N
120° 10' 00" Lon - W

Lake Definition (No. 3 Lake)

Elevation: 1,066.8 m (3,425 ft)
Surface Area: 6.1 ha (94 ac)
Mean Depth: 4.3 m (24.4 ft)
Max Depth: 8.2 m (45 ft)
Perimeter: 3,994 m (13,100 ft)

Thompson Nicola Region

Little Fort
Sicamous
Salmon Arm
Clinton
Cache Creek
Kamloops
Gold Bridge
Lillooet
Merritt
Bleeker Lake
Boston Bar
Spuzzum

Map Courtesy of Backroad Mapbook Volume III Kamloops/Okanagan

Scale

100m   0   100m   200m   300m   400m   500m

— Scale —

Bleeker Lake

To Hwy 5A

To Campbell Lake

No. 3 Lake

Recent Fish Stocking (Bleeker)

Year	Fish Species	Life Stage	Number
1999	rainbow trout	YE	3,000
1998	rainbow trout	YE	3,000
1997	rainbow trout	YE	3,000
1996	rainbow trout	YE	3,000
1995	rainbow trout	YE	3,000

Bluey Lake

To Hwy 97C

Bluey Lake Rec Site

To Hwy 5A

6m
18
12m
15
12m
12m
6

N

Access/Parking

Bluey Lakes is found south of the beautiful Kentucky-Alleyne Recreation Area. The area is highlighted by open range land with encroaching forests. Several small lakes dot the landscape. The lakes in the area are popular throughout the summer months given the good fishing and the scenic surroundings. There are several different lakes to choose from in the area with Bluey, Alleyne and Kentucky Lakes being the focus of most of the fishing activity.

To reach Bluey Lake, take the Bates Road, a good 2wd road. Bates Road can either be accessed by heading southwest from the Loon Lake interchange on the Okanagan Connector or by heading south on Highway #5 from the Aspen Grove Interchange and taking a left once you reach Bates Road turn-off. Once on Bates Road, you will soon reach the north end of Kentucky Lake so long as you remain on the main road.

Bluey Lake is located south of Kentucky Lake on a rough 4wd road which is probably best left to hiking especially in wetter conditions. The road leads from Bates Road a few hundred meters to the west of Kentucky Lake.

Bluey Lake can also be accessed off of the Missezula Lake Road. An old 4wd road reaches the south end of Bluey Lake from that road.

Fishing

With the poor access, Bluey Lake does not receive the same fishing pressure as other lakes in the area. Because of this and the existence of an intensive stocking program, the lake now offers good fishing for small rainbow. Some of the rainbow do reach the 1-2 kg (2-6 lbs) range, however.

The lake has several holes 12-18 m (40-60 ft) deep, one at the south end, one at the west end and one at the east end of the lake. There is a nice shoal area in the middle of the lake near the two small islands. Try fly fishing or spincasting off these shoals for best results. The usual hatches happen at the lake (damselfly; dragonfly, mayfly, chironomid and sedge).

Trolling is seldom tried at the lake because of the poor access and difficulty getting a decent boat into the lake. Also, the lake has limited deep areas so trollers often hang-up making fishing rather frustrating

Spinners and lures like the Mepps, Blue Fox and Flatfish are worth trying with a worm.

Fishing is best after ice-off (mid-May) and again late in the fall. The reason being, the waters tend to warm given the shallow waters.

Facilities

There is a rec site at the north end of the lake that offers 12 camping spots and a cartop boat launch. Kentucky Lake also offers a 63 vehicle/tent campsite.

Other Options

The Kentucky-Alleyne Recreation Area, to the north offers several different options including **Alleyne**, **Crater** and **Kentucky Lakes**. These lakes are highlighted in this book.

Another good alternative is **Missezula Lake** to the south. This large 259 ha lake has good access and receives heavy fishing pressure. Try in the spring and fall for the stocked rainbow and brook trout, which can reach 2 kg (5 lbs). Trollers also hook into a few kokanee.

Lake Definition

Elevation:	1,036.3 m (3,400 ft)
Surface Area:	29.8 ha (73.7 ac)
Mean Depth:	12 m (39.4 ft)
Max Depth:	17.7 m (58 ft)
Perimeter:	6,001.6 m (19,690 ft)
Way Point:	49° 52' 00" Lat - N
	120° 34' 00" Lon - W

100m   0   100m   200m   300m   400m

Scale

100m   200m   300m

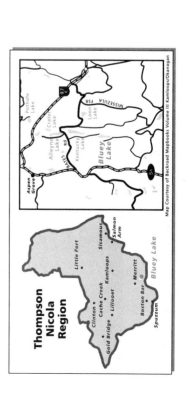

Map Courtesy of Backroad Mapbooks Volume III Kamloops/Okanagan

Aspen Grove
Pothole Lake
Crater Lake
Alleyne Lake
Bates Rd
Kentucky Lake
Loon Lake
MISSEZULA FSR
Bluey Lake

Thompson Nicola Region

Little Fort
Sicamous
Salmon Arm
Clinton
Cache Creek
Kamloops
Lillooet
Merritt
Gold Bridge
Boston Bar
Spuzzum
Bluey Lake

Bolean Lake

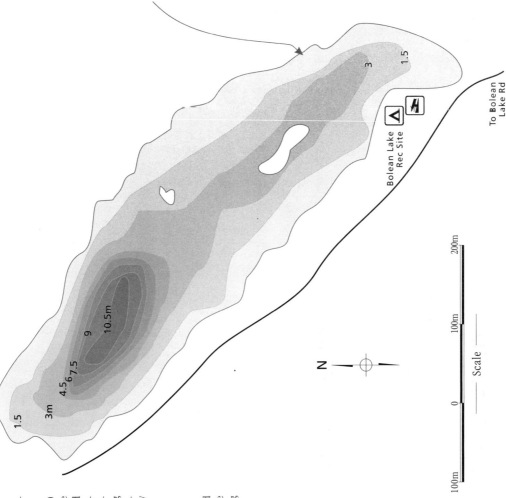

To Bolean
Lake Rd

Bolean Lake
Rec Site

N

Scale

100m   0   100m   200m

Access/Parking

Bolean Lake is one of three lakes found at the top of Spa Hills northeast of Falkland. To reach Bolean Lake, simply drive south on Highway #97 from Falkland. Soon, you will see a mainhaul logging road called the Bolean Lake Road, which leads to the left. The road brings you directly to Bolean Lake. A 2wd vehicle is sufficient.

Fishing

This 70 ha lake is rather unique as it has a pothole at the northwestern end of the lake that is 10.5 m (35 ft) deep. The rest of the lake is rather shallow (less than 3 m /10 ft deep) but you wouldn't know it as the water is a tea colour. The fishing season for rainbow runs from May to October with good action during the summer months. There are a lot of small rainbow but you may be able to hook a 1.5 kg (3 lb) fish if you are lucky. If fly fishing, an attractor type fly is your best bet. Cast near the drop-off around the pothole except in early spring and late fall when the fish are cruising the shallows. Spincasters should use small lures with bait.

The lake is not that suitable for trolling given the large shallows. If you plan to troll, stick around the pothole and use a wedding band or small lure with a worm.

Facilities

There is a campground, some cabins and a store in addition to a rec site at the lake.

The Bolean Lake Lodge (250-558-9908 or www.bcfroa.bc.ca) offers lakeside cabins with wood cook stoves, kitchenware but no linen or fridge. There is a central washroom and shower (except the deluxe cabins) and power is via a generator. Limited camping is also available for a fee. In addition, there is a store stocking basic groceries and fishing tackle, a boat launch and rowboat & power boat rentals. Similar to the fishing season, the lodge is open from May 15 to October 15.

Other Options

Arthur and **Spa Lake** are found to the east and offer good fly fishing in tea coloured water. Due to the elevation, these lakes are most productive in early June. Rainbow to 1.5 kg (3 lbs) are best taken on a fly.

Both lakes offer recreation sites and boat launches.

Lake Definition

Elevation:	4,753 m (15,593.6 ft)
Surface Area:	78 ha (192.7 ac)
Mean Depth:	3.4 m (11.2 ft)
Max Depth:	12 m (39.4 ft)
Perimeter:	4,753m (15,594 ft)
Way Point:	50° 32' 00" Lat - N
	126° 25' 00" Lon - W

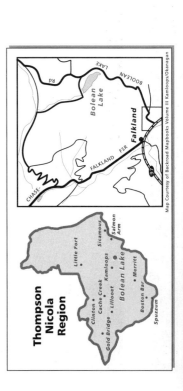

Thompson Nicola Region

Little Fort
Sicamous
Salmon Arm
Cache Creek
Kamloops
Clinton
Lillooet
Bolean Lake
Gold Bridge
Merritt
Boston Bar
Spuzzum

Bonaparte Lake

Access/Parking

Bonaparte Lake is a large, cold lake, which is located at the northern end of the Bonaparte Plateau. A spruce, pine, and subalpine fir forest typical for the plateau surrounds the lake.

To reach the lake really depends on where you are coming from and where you are going. Regardless, it is a long drive on gravel roads. It is a good idea to bring a copy of the Backroad Mapbook Volume III Kamloops/Okanagan before trying to untangle the web of roads to find your way to Bonaparte Lake.

From either Highway 24 or 97, find the North Bonaparte Road and continue to the Rayfield River. Look for the Egan-Bonaparte Forest Service Road (3700 Rd) heading south. That road will eventually bring you to the west end of the lake after many dusty, teeth rattling miles on a mainhaul logging road.

To approach Bonaparte Lake from the east, head north on Highway #5 past Barriére and take the Boulder Mountain Road to the right. If you reach Chinook Cove on Highway #5 you have gone too far. Once on Boulder Mountain Road, the only major intersection is the Bonaparte Forest Service Road. This road leads off to the west and slowly winds its way to the east end of the lake.

Fishing

Bonaparte Lake has large rainbow in the 5.5 kg (12 lbs) range which feast on the abundant kokanee in the lake. However, most of the fish are in the 1-1.5 kg (3-4 lbs) range.

Trolling is the mainstay of the lake with plugs and Krocodile lures working the best when trolled deep (10-30 m/30-90 ft). Fly fishermen will have a very difficult time catching anything as the rainbow just don't seem to be attracted to any fly pattern.

Trolling a Spin N Glo or Willow Leaf with maggots easily catches the small kokanee. A Dick Nite also works for the kokanee. Fishing remains active throughout the summer months but is best in early spring or late fall. Ice fishing with bait and a hook is very productive.

Be warned the lake is susceptible to sudden, strong winds and big waves.

Lake Definition

Elevation: 1,169 m (3834 ft)
Surface Area: 33,674 ha (83,175 ac)
Mean Depth: 40.3 m (131 ft)
Max Depth: 98 m (321 ft)
Perimeter: 41,450 m (135,956 ft)
Way Point: 51° 15' 00" Lat - N
120° 34' 00" Lon - W

Facilities

Bonaparte Lake has several resorts to choice from together with the **Bonaparte Lake Rec Site**, which is located at the northwest end of the lake. The rec site contains a good boat launch together with several camping sites in a forested area. The campsite offers little privacy and no view.

Bonaparte Lake Resort has a campground and RV hook-ups (10 units) as well as 7 cabins complete with fridge, stove and washroom. Central showers, store, boat launch and boat rentals are also offered at the resort.

Thunderbird Lodge (250-371-9946) has 7 lakeside cabins with electricity, flush toilets, fridge and running water. A 16 unit campground with electric and water hook-up is also available for a fee. There are also central showers, smokehouse, boat rentals and a store at the resort.

Other Options

The Bonaparte Plateau offers literally hundreds of lakes to sample. **Lupin Lakes** to the east offer a unique opportunity to combine a backcountry canoe trip with good rainbow fishing. **Allan** and **Mayson Lakes** are other popular options to the west. To the west, be sure to check out **Hammer** and **Scot Lakes**.

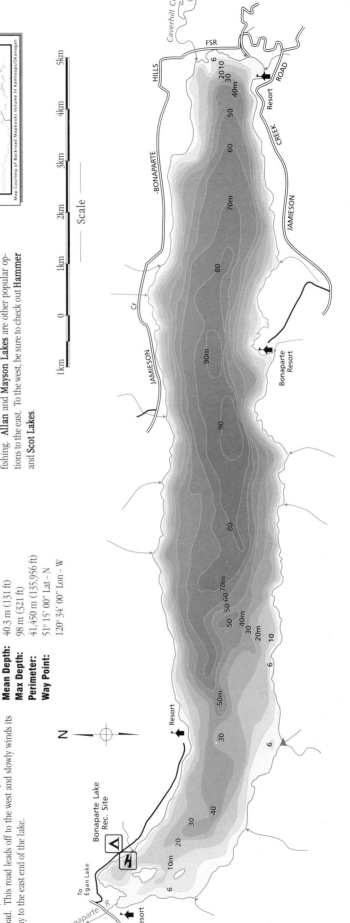

Thompson Nicola Region

Map Courtesy of Backroad Mapbooks Volume III Kamloops/Okanagan

Campbell Lake

Map Courtesy of Backroad Mapbooks Volume III Kamloops/Okanagan

Access/Parking

Campbell Lake is a 90 ha lake located next to the tiny community of Bestwick in the heart of rangeland. Since the lake is surrounded by private property, be sure to obtain permission before crossing private land.

The lake is best reached by taking the Barnhartvale Road from the Trans Canada Highway east of Kamloops. Continue past the community of Barnhartvale to the Robins-Campbell Range Road and that main logging road will take you south to Bestwick and the lake.

It is possible to reach Campbell Lake from the south by taking the Roche Lake Road from Highway #5A and then when you reach the Roche Lake Provincial Park, take a right at the Bleeker Lake Road. Hang on as you pound your way north on the rough road leading past Bleeker, Hosli and Scuitto Lakes before finally reaching Campbell Lake.

There are several other ways to reach Campbell Lake as there is a vast network of interconnecting logging roads. It is well advised to grab your Backroad Mapbook Volume III Kamloops/Okanagan before trying to untangle the web of roads to find your way to Campbell Lake.

Once you reach the lake, accesses is through private property owned by the Campbell Lake Ranch so get permission before you head to the lake.

Fishing

Campbell Lake is a shallow, nutrient rich lake, which has a small dam. There are three deep pockets (22 m/70 ft) scattered throughout the lake, one at the east and two near the middle of the lake. The rest of the lake is only 8-12 m (25-40 ft) deep but you wouldn't know it as the water is dark and filled with plankton so you cannot see the bottom. As a result, a depth chart is extremely important so you c a n read this lake and know where to fish.

Campbell is stocked annually with rainbow trout that can reach 5 kg (10-12 lbs) in size but average 1.5 kg (2-3 lbs). The lake is considered a very good fly fishing lake for the skilled angler especially in the late spring during the caddisfly hatch. Damselfly and dragonfly patterns cast near the reeds can be dynamite given that the fish move into the shallows to feed.

The lake suffers from a thick algae bloom in the summer so fishing is very difficult at that time of year. Also, the lake is susceptible to windy conditions during the summer further complicating fishing. It is not until the late fall that fishing picks up again once the algae bloom begins to retreat.

Please note that the lake is closed to fishing from Dec 1-April 30, there is a two trout limit and you must use single barbless hooks.

Facilities

There are no developed facilities at the lake and the lake is surrounded by private property. If you want to camp at the lake then get permission from the private property owners.

Other Options

Nearby **Scuitto Lake** provides good fly fishing for rainbow that average under 2 kg (5 lbs) in size but can reach 5 kg (10 lbs). A 2wd road off the Bestwick Road accesses the shallow lake.

Hosli Lake, accessed by 4wd vehicle, is stocked annually with rainbow trout that can reach 2+ kg (5 lbs) in size.

Lake Definition

Elevation:	1,066 m (3,497 ft)
Surface Area:	113.2 ha (279.6 ac)
Mean Depth:	2 m (6.6 ft)
Max Depth:	5.5 m (18 ft)
Perimeter:	8,800m (28,871 ft)
Way Point:	50° 33' 00" Lat - N
	123° 05' 00" Lon - W

Recent Fish Stocking

Year	Fish Species	Life Stage	Number
1998	rainbow trout	YE	5,500
1997	rainbow trout	YE	5,500
1996	rainbow trout	YE	5,500
1995	rainbow trout	YE	5,500

Scale
200m 0 200m 400m 600m 800m 1000m

To Beswick

To Scuitto Lake

Caverhill Lake

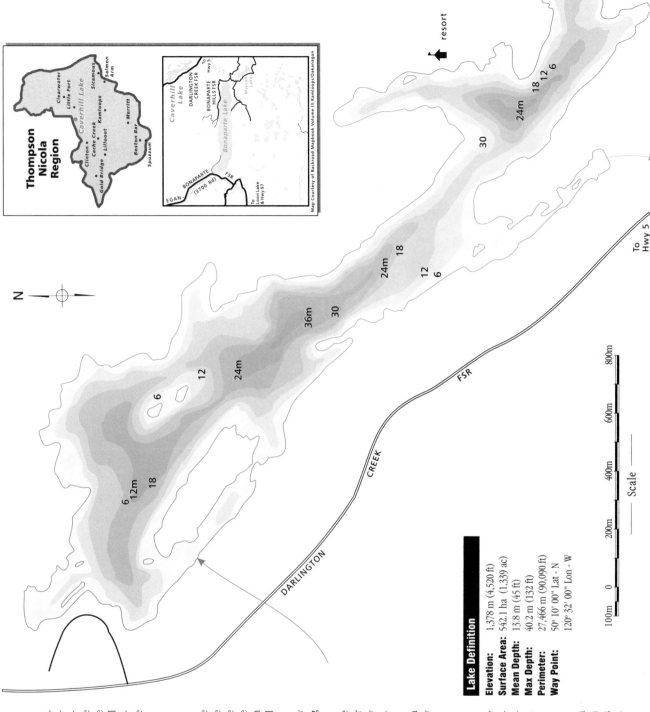

Thompson Nicola Region

Clearwater
Little Fort
Caverhill Lake
Sicamous
Salmon Arm
Clinton
Cache Creek
Kamloops
Gold Bridge
Lillooet
Merritt
Boston Bar
Spuzzum

To Hwy 5
Caverhill Lake
DARLINGTON CREEK FSR
BONAPARTE HILLS FSR
Mahood Lake
Bonaparte Lake
EGAN
BONAPARTE (3700 Rd) FSR
To Loon Lake & Hwy 97

Map Courtesy of Backroad Mapbook Volume III Kamloops/Okanagan

N

resort

6m
12m
18
6
12
24m
36m
30
24m
18
12
6
30
24m
18
12
6

DARLINGTON CREEK FSR

To Hwy 5

100m 0 200m 400m 600m 800m
Scale

Lake Definition

Elevation: 1,378 m (4,520 ft)
Surface Area: 542.1 ha (1,339 ac)
Mean Depth: 13.8 m (45 ft)
Max Depth: 40.2 m (132 ft)
Perimeter: 27,466 m (90,090 ft)
Way Point: 50° 10' 00" Lat - N
120° 32' 00" Lon - W

Access/Parking

Just north of Darfield on Highway #5 (south of Little Fort), a main haul logging road called the Darlington Creek Forest Service Road heads westward. The road winds up a series of switchbacks out of the Thompson River Valley to the Bonaparte Plateau. At 6.3 km, take the left branch of the road and after a total of 23 dust filled kilometers, you will reach the south end of the lake. The Darlington Creek Forest Service Road continues along the western shore of the lake.

Fishing

Caverhill Lake is one of the larger lakes in the Bonaparte Plateau but the many bays and arms give the appearance of a small, fly fishermen friendly lake. The ice leaves the lake by mid-May and the open water fishing runs all the way to the end of October. Since the lake does not warm significantly in the summer months, fast fishing for small trout is common for the entire ice-free season.

The rainbow can grow to 1 kg (2 lbs) and are best fished by trolling a small lure such as a Flatfish or Deadly Dick. Gang trolls also produce.

Fly fishing is a tough sell at this lake due to the fact that the lake does not have the prolific hatches common to other Thompson/Nicola lakes. If that doesn't discourage you, try a chironomid pupa, mayfly nymph, sedge or leech pattern. A Tom Tom fly is a local favorite.

100,000 kokanee were stocked in the lake in 1991. To catch the small kokanee, troll a Wedding Ring or pink lure slowly at 5-8 m (15-25 ft).

Facilities

The Caverhill Resort (250-672-9806) is a boat access only resort open from June to October. The resort has rustic cabins, boat launch, boat rentals and camping. The resort provides a base camp for the surrounding lakes like Akehurst.

Other Options

Akehurst Lake is located west of Caverhill Lake and has a similar fishery as Caverhill Lake. It also has a resort with cabins, boats and a restaurant. There are also numerous hike-in lakes in the area offering fast action for small rainbow on a fly.

Chapperon Lake

Access/Parking

Chapperon Lake is a private lake found in the heart of cattle country and the Douglas Lake Ranch. From Merritt, drive along Highway #5A past Nicola Lake and take a right on the Douglas Lake Road. This good access road will take you past Douglas Lake with the next major lake being Chapperon Lake. An access road leading south of Douglas Lake Road conveniently circles the lake.

Fishing

Chapperon is a very shallow lake with the maximum depth only 5 m (20 ft). Thus, the lake is subject to winterkill.

The lake is known to contain a lot of rainbow trout, which can reach 2 kg (5 lbs). Fly fishing is an excellent way to sample this waterbody. The shallow water allows a proliferation of insect growth and there is plenty of food for the rainbow. Try to match one of the hatches. In the fall, backswimmer, leech and Doc Spratley patterns work well.

Trolling is not possible as the lake is simply too shallow to troll effectively. The summer doldrums are a real problem given that the waters warm significantly in the heat of the summer.

Facilities

There are no developed facilities at the lake.

Other Options

The Douglas Lake Road provides good access to several other lakes. **Douglas Lake** offers rainbow and small kokanee, primarily by trolling in the spring. Another popular lake found northeast of Chapperon Lake is **Salmon Lake**, this lake is better described later in this book.

Call Douglas Lake Ranch at 1-800-663-4838 for more information on fishing within the ranch.

Lake Definition

Elevation:	930 m (3,050 ft)
Surface Area:	393.4 ha (972 ac)
Mean Depth:	2.4 m (7.9 ft)
Max Depth:	5 m (16.4 ft)
Perimeter:	13,440 m (4,408 ft)
Way Point:	50° 12' 00" Lat - N
	120° 03' 00" Lon - W

To Westwold
(Hwy 97)

LAKE

Rd

DOUGLAS

To
Douglas
Lake

1
2m
3
4m

200m 0   200m 400m 600m 800m 1000m

—— Scale ——

Map Courtesy of Backroad Mapbooks Volume III Kamloops/Okanagan

To Westwold

Index
Lake

Pikehead
Lake

Nauchachapt
Lake

LAKE

Rd

DOUGLAS

Chapperon
Lake

To Douglas
Lake

Thompson Nicola Region

Little Fort
Sicamous
Salmon Arm
Clinton
Cache Creek
Kamloops
Lillooet
Chapperon Lake
Merritt
Gold Bridge
Boston Bar
Spuzzum

Corbett Lake

Access/Parking

Corbett Lake is found in the centre of a 123 ha private ranch and is managed for the guests of the Corbett Lake Country Inn. Visitors to the area can fish the lake for a fee. The area surrounding the lake is renown for its open rolling hills, meadows of wildflowers and numerous lakes. The lake, at 1070 m in elevation, is quite shallow and contains clear water, which allows you to see the drop-offs.

To reach Corbett Lake, simply drive 18.5 km southeast from Merritt on the Okanagan Connector (Hwy 97C). The 20 ha lake is located right next to the Okanagan Connector at the junction with the Kane Valley Rd.

Facilities

The Corbett Lake Country Inn (250-378-4434) offers cedar cottages, with full kitchens and fireplaces as well as accommodation in the main lodge. Peter McVey, the owner, prides himself on fine dining with four course meals a regular event. The accommodations are reasonable and row boats are available for rent. If you need some casting instruction or local fishing advise, Peter is certainly there to help.

A small parking lot and cartop boat launch is located at the north end of the lake away from the resort and next to the Okanagan Connector.

Fishing

Corbett Lake is a fly fishing only lake, which offers reasonably good fishing in the spring and fall for rainbow. The fish average 1 kg (2 lbs) but range in size from 0.5 lbs to 6-3 kg (7 lbs) and are usually short and fat. By far the best time to fish is during the mayfly and chironomid hatches in May- June. If you are trying the chironomid hatch a dark green or black patterns is a killer. Damselfly patterns such as a #8 olive green pattern can also produce.

The lake has many weed covered shoals and nice drop-offs. A large marshy shallow and shoal area is located at the west and east end of the lake whereas the north and south shores drop-off a lot quicker. Focus you efforts off the east and west end of the lake where the water begins to get deep.

The lake is stocked annually with rainbow to ensure reasonable success for the fishermen while maintaining a

Other Options

Courtney Lake and the **Kane Valley Lakes** are found close by and provide a good alternative. Look for their descriptions in this book.

Lake Definition

Elevation:	1,042 m (3,417.8 ft)
Surface Area:	29 ha (71.8 ac)
Mean Depth:	6.2 m (20.3 ft)
Max Depth:	20.3 m (66.6 ft)
Perimeter:	3,040 m (9,971.2 ft)
Way Point:	50° 01' 25" Lat - N
	120° 37' 10" Lon - W

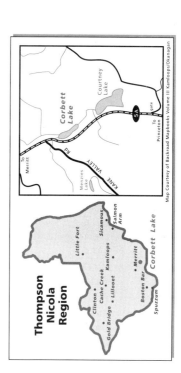

Thompson Nicola Region

Map Courtesy of Backroad Mapbooks Volume III Kamloops/Okanagan

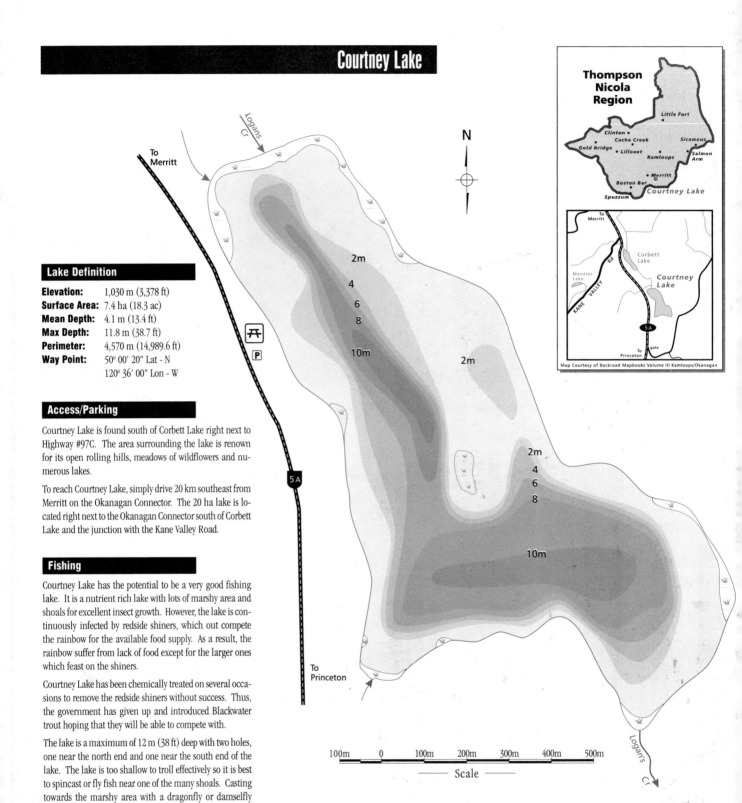

Thompson Nicola Region

Map Courtesy of Backroad Mapbooks Volume III Kamloops/Okanagan

Lake Definition

Elevation: 1,030 m (3,378 ft)
Surface Area: 7.4 ha (18.3 ac)
Mean Depth: 4.1 m (13.4 ft)
Max Depth: 11.8 m (38.7 ft)
Perimeter: 4,570 m (14,989.6 ft)
Way Point: 50° 00' 20" Lat - N
120° 36' 00" Lon - W

Access/Parking

Courtney Lake is found south of Corbett Lake right next to Highway #97C. The area surrounding the lake is renown for its open rolling hills, meadows of wildflowers and numerous lakes.

To reach Courtney Lake, simply drive 20 km southeast from Merritt on the Okanagan Connector. The 20 ha lake is located right next to the Okanagan Connector south of Corbett Lake and the junction with the Kane Valley Road.

Fishing

Courtney Lake has the potential to be a very good fishing lake. It is a nutrient rich lake with lots of marshy area and shoals for excellent insect growth. However, the lake is continuously infected by redside shiners, which out compete the rainbow for the available food supply. As a result, the rainbow suffer from lack of food except for the larger ones which feast on the shiners.

Courtney Lake has been chemically treated on several occasions to remove the redside shiners without success. Thus, the government has given up and introduced Blackwater trout hoping that they will be able to compete with.

The lake is a maximum of 12 m (38 ft) deep with two holes, one near the north end and one near the south end of the lake. The lake is too shallow to troll effectively so it is best to spincast or fly fish near one of the many shoals. Casting towards the marshy area with a dragonfly or damselfly nymph works very well. Also, minnow imitations can produce. In the fall try a Courtney special, leech, muddler minnow or dragon fly patterns.

Any spoon or lure that imitates the minnows may produce a lunker (3+ kg/6+ lb). A Blue Fox, Deadly Dick, silver Flatfish or Krocodile are worth casting.

The summer doldrums are at their best at this lake so try in the early spring or late fall.

The lake has a one trout limit, single barbless hook restriction, bait ban and an ice fishing ban.

Facilities

There is a road side parking area for day use. Camping is possible in the Kane Valley and there is a resort on Corbett Lake.

Other Options

See **Corbett Lake** and the **Kane Valley Chain Lakes**, which are described in this book.

Recent Fish Stocking

Year	Fish Species	Life Stage	Number
1999	rainbow trout	YE	3,000
1998	rainbow trout	YE	2,000
1996	rainbow trout	FG, YE	3,006
1995	rainbow trout	YE	1,000

Crystal Lake

Access/Parking

The best and least nerve racking way to reach Crystal Lake is to drive to Bridge Lake on Hwy #24 and then take the North Bonaparte Road south to Crystal Lake. The lake is 4 km southwest of the Bridge Lake Store.

Fishing

Crystal Lake offers reasonably good fishing for rainbow trout that average under 1.2 lbs (0.5 kg) in size but can reach 4.5 lbs (2 kg) in size. The lake has clear water and is best suited for float tubes, rowboats and canoes. The lake produces well beginning after ice-off in the early part of May and the fishing remains good until into the early part of the summer. The summer doldrums soon hit and the fishing falls off until late September.

There is no really clear choice as to how to fish the lake. You will see trollers, spincasters and fly fishermen hooking on to the trout. If you are flyfishing, use a long leader because of the clear water and match the hatch. Chironomid, midge, sedge, dragonfly and damselfly patterns all produce depending on the hatch.

Facilities

There is a rec site at the west side of the lake with a cartop boat launch and 7 camping sites. The site is nicely treed and located next to the lake. It can be reached by cars and RVs.

The Crystal Waters Guest Ranch (1-888-593-2252 or cwranch@bcadventure.com) is found at the west end of Crystal Lake and has log cabins with electric heat offered at $108-$136 per night. The guest ranch has a central washroom, showers and laundry as well as a recreation lodge and dining room.

Lake Definition

Elevation: 1,159 m (3,801 ft)
Surface Area: 138.3 ha (341 ac)
Mean Depth: 23 m (75 ft)
Max Depth: 18 m (59 ft)
Perimeter: 7,150 m (23,452 sq ft)
Way Point: 51° 27' 30" Lat - N
120° 45' 30" Lon - W

Other Options

Highway 24 gives access to an endless number of good fishing lakes. **Bridge Lake** is a large lake that is best trolled. The lake offers stocked rainbow and kokanee as well as some large lake trout (to 6 kg/13 lbs). The smaller lakes surrounding Crystal lake can also produce small trout on a fly.

Recent Fish Stocking

Year	Fish Species	Life Stage	Number
1999	rainbow trout	YE	40,000
1998	rainbow trout	YE	25,000
1997	rainbow trout	YE, FR	37,500
1996	rainbow trout	YE, FF	30,052
1995	rainbow trout	YE	20,000

To Bridge Lake & Hwy 24

N

Crystal Lake Recreation Site

BONAPARTE Rd

NORTH

To North Bonaparte & 70 Mile House

18m 16 14 12 10m 8 6 4 2m

100m 0 100m 200m 300m 400m 500m
Scale

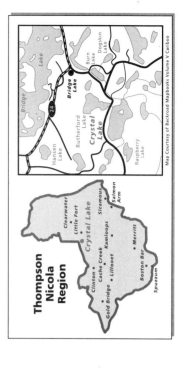

Thompson Nicola Region

Clearwater
Little Fort
Crystal Lake
Salmon Arm
Sicamous
Clinton
Cache Creek
Kamloops
Gold Bridge
Lilloet
Merritt
Boston Bar
Spuzzum

Bridge Lake
Burn Lake
Dogskin Lake
24
Bridge Lake
Rutherford Lake
Hansen Lake
Crystal Lake
Raspberry Lake

Map Courtesy of Backroad Mapbooks Volume V Cariboo

Cultus (Baldwin) Lake

Access/Parking

This 34 ha lake is located northwest of Savona and is easily accessed by the Deadman-Cache Creek Road.

To reach the lake, head west from Savona on the Trans Canada Highway. The third major logging road heading north from the Trans-Canada is the Battle Creek Forest Service Road. Follow that road along the eastern boundary of the Arrowstone Provincial Park to the junction with the Deadman-Cache Creek Road. Take a right and you will soon pass Stinking Lake before reaching Cultus Lake.

An alternative, longer route is to drive the Deadman-Vidette Road along the Deadman River until your reach the Deadman-Cache Creek Road junction. Hang a left and the road will soon reach the northern shores of Cultus Lake.

Fishing

Cultus Lake is a fairly shallow lake (maximum depth 12 m/39 ft) with an extensive marshy area at the north end. The lake also has some decent shoals around its entire length. The fishing for small trout begins in early May and slows in the summertime due to the summer algae bloom. Later in the fall is also a good time to fish.

Although it is possible to troll, the depth of the lake makes fly fishing and spincasting more productive. You will find most of the insect hatches of the Thompson/Nicola Region at this lake.

Other Options

Stinking Lake is a shallow lake (6-9 m/20-30 ft) offering good fishing for brook trout in the spring and fall. Try spincasting with bait and fishing near the bottom. Good access is provided along the Deadman-Cache Creek Road. Brook trout are stocked every two years.

Lake Definition

Elevation:	838 m (2,750 ft)
Surface Area:	38 ha (94.8 ac)
Mean Depth:	5.8 m (19 ft)
Max Depth:	11.3 m (37 ft)
Perimeter:	4,023.4 m (15,200 ft)
Way Point:	50° 52' 00" Lat - N
	121° 03' 00" Lon - W

Facilities

There are no developed facilities at Cultus Lake. It is possible to camp along the lakeshore next to the logging roads that pass by the northern and southern shores of the lake.

Launching a cartop boat is also possible.

N

To Deadman Vidette Rd

ROAD

CREEK

-CACHE

DEADMAN

3 6 9m

To Cache Creek

Thompson Nicola Region

Clearwater
Little Fort
Cultus Lake
Sicamous
Salmon Arm
Cache Creek
Kamloops
Clinton
Merritt
Gold Bridge
Lillooet
Boston Bar
Spuzzum

DEADMAN VIDETTE Rd

Rd

CACHE CREEK

Cultus Lake

Stinking Lake

BATTLE CREEK FSR

Thompson River

Scale

200m 0   400m   800m   1200m   1600m   2000m

Deadman Lake

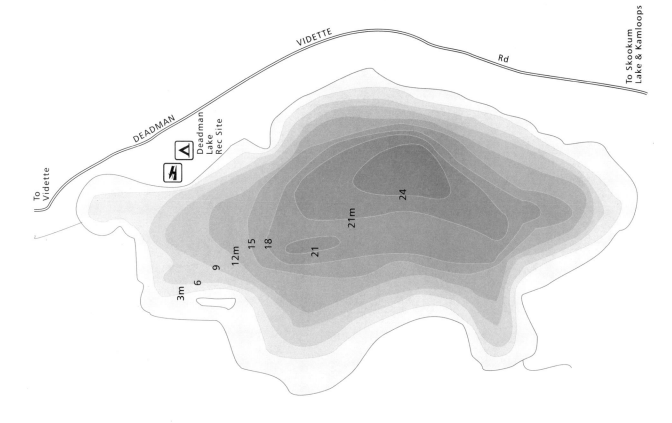

Access/Parking

Do not be discouraged by the name or the remote access as this lake can be very productive.

To reach the lake, take the Deadman-Vidette Road leading north from the Trans Canada Highway just west of the Deadman River Bridge. The road follows the Deadman River for what appears like an eternity until you reach Skookum Lake. Beyond, Skookum Lake, it is well advised that you have a 4wd vehicle, as the road is extremely rough.

It is also possible to reach the lake from Highway #97 by taking the Clinton-Loon Lake Road to Vidette. Head south past Vidette Lake and you will soon reach Deadman Lake on the Deadman-Vidette Road.

It is a good idea to bring a copy of the Backroad Mapbook Volume III Kamloops/Okanagan before trying to access Deadman Lake.

Fishing

Deadman Lake is 20 ha in size and has reasonably good fishing for rainbow and kokanee that reach 1 kg (2 lbs) in size. The lake is fairly deep (25 m/80 ft) and so it is easily trolled. Nice fertile shoals are located near the north and south ends of the lake as well as around the island at the southeast end of the lake.

Trollers should use a Willow Leaf for both the rainbow and kokanee. Some of the smaller lures such as a Flatfish, Dick Nite or Krocodile also work for the rainbow. Pink lures such as the Spin-N-Glow take kokanee.

Fly fishermen should focus their efforts around the shoals and the nice drop-offs. Most of the insect hatches common to the region are also found at this lake so try matching one of the hatches.

The thick forest surrounding the lake makes it tough to cast from shore so a float tube or boat is definitely a benefit. The lake, given its elevation and depth, has a reasonably good fishery during the summer months.

Facilities

The Deadman Lake Rec Site is located on the eastern shore and offers 10 treed camping sites together with tables, pit toilets and a cartop boat launch.

Other Options

Skookum, **Snohoosh** and **Vidette Lakes** are found within close proximity of Deadman Lake. All lakes are highlighted in this book.

Lake Definition

Elevation: 816.8 m (2,680 ft)
Surface Area: 49.4 ha (122 ac)
Mean Depth: 11.7 m (38.3 ft)
Max Depth: 24.9 m (82 ft)
Perimeter: 3,380.3 m (11,040 ft)
Way Point: 49° 57' 00" Lat - N
123° 32' 00" Lon - W

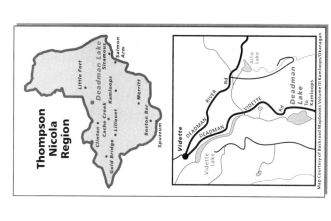

Thompson Nicola Region

Map Courtesy of Backroad Mapbooks Volume III Kamloops/Okanagan

Desmond Lake

Access/Parking

Desmond Lake is situated in a rolling lodgepole forest common to the Lac Le Jeune area. The weedy shoreline and inviting shoals of the lake often entice fishermen traveling the Coquihalla Highway.

Take Exit 336 between Merritt and Kamloops on the Coquihalla Highway (Lac Le Jeune/ Logan Lake Exit) and head west on the paved, Meadow Creek Road. The first major intersection to the left is the signed, Surrey Lake Forest Service Road. Follow that washboard gravel road south for 3 km and you will see the lake on your left.

A short walk to the lake and you are fishing.

Fishing

Desmond Lake has the type of terrain ideal for a great fly fishing lake. It has three distinct potholes, one at the west end of the lake and two towards the east end of the lake. There are also some nice shoals particularly near the east and west ends of the lake. However, Desmond Lake has spotty fishing for rainbow trout which grow to 1 kg (2-3 lbs).

The lake is best fished by trolling using a gang troll or fly (Leech, Doc Spratley or Carey Special). Focus on the edges of the deep potholes particularly during the summer months when the fish retreat to the depths of Lake.

With the number of drop-offs and shoals, the lake offer plenty of areas for fly fishermen and spincasters to focus. Fly fishermen can use damselfly nymphs, dragonfly nymphs, mayflies or chironomids. A Mepp, Panther Martin or Blue Fox is worth casting.

Facilities

There are no developed facilities at the lake but you can certainly camp in the grasslands near the lake or stay at the nearby Surrey Lake Fishing Camp.

Lake Definition

Surface Area: 25 ha (61.8 ac)
Mean Depth: 3.2 m (10.5 ft)
Max Depth: 9.1 m (30 ft)
Perimeter: 2,500 m (8,202 ft)
Way Point: 50° 26' 00" Lat - N
120° 37' 00" Lon - W

Other Options

To the south of Desmond Lake along the Surrey Lake Forest Service Road is **Surrey Lake**. It is a slightly larger lake offering better fishing than Desmond Lake. The popular fishing lake has murky water making it difficult to see the shoals and weed beds. Most fishermen focus their efforts off the weed beds right in front of the Surrey Lake Fishing Camp or they fish in front of the private cabin located on the tip of the small peninsula. The lake produces very well by trolling a Willow Leaf and worm or a green, yellow or froggy Kwikfish (K4 size). Fly fishermen seem to do best with green imitations such as a green Carey or green half back. A small black coloured, dry fly cast towards the shallows near dusk is excellent. The rainbow are generally under 0.5 kg (1 lb) but can reach 3 kg (6-7 lbs).

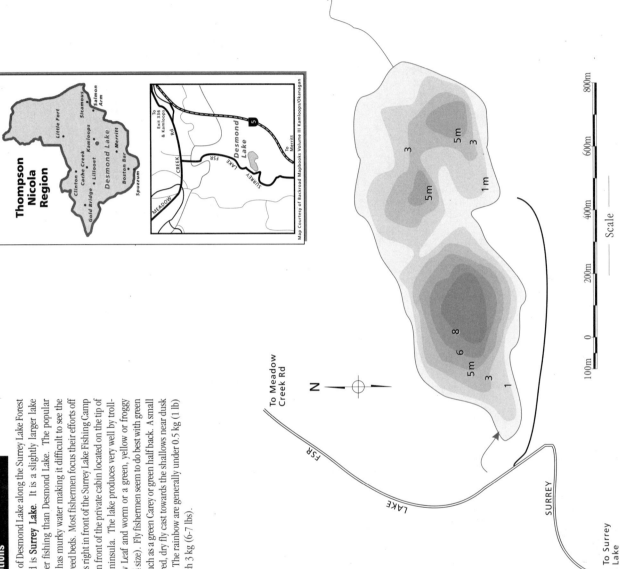

Map Courtesy of Backroad Mapbooks Volume III Kamloops/Okanagan

Duffy Lake

Access/Parking

This 25 ha lake is located on the Duffy Lake Road south of the little community of Cherry Creek. To reach the lake, head west on Highway #1 from Kamloops past the Highway #5 interchange. About 6 km later, the Dominic Lake Road leads to the south. The second major intersection leading to the west on the Dominic Lake Road is the Duffy Lake Road. That road is accessible via a 4wd vehicle.

Fishing

The lake is stocked annually with rainbow that can reach 2 kg (5 lbs) in size although the average fish is quite small. It is 11 m (36 ft) deep and has nice drop-offs and shoals ideal for fly fishing and spincasting. Both trolling and fly fishing are popular although fly fishing is definitely more productive. That is because the water is clear and the fish tend to spook when a boat motor passes by. Since the lake is fairly high in elevation (1160 m/3805 ft), the summer fishery remains quite productive.

For the fly fishermen, try a shrimp, dragonfly or mayfly pattern depending on the hatch.

Facilities

Duffy Lake Rec Site has 30 camping units together with a cartop boat launch.

Other Options

South of Duffy Lake lies a series of good fishing lakes. A couple lakes are worth mentioning:

Dairy Lake is a heavily stocked lake, which is subject to summer draw-down and winter-kill. Trolling and fly fishing should produce average size rainbow.

Dominic Lake is a resort lake that offers good fishing for rainbow to 1 kg (2 lbs).

Lake Definition

Elevation: 1,158.5 m (3,800 ft)
Surface Area: 23 ha (58 ac)
Mean Depth: 6.7 m (22 ft)
Max Depth: 10.9 m (36 ft)
Perimeter: 2,417.7 m (7,932 ft)
Way Point: 50° 39' 00" Lat - N
120° 43' 00" Lon - W

Recent Fish Stocking

Year	Fish Species	Life Stage	Number
1997	rainbow trout	YE	3,500
1996	rainbow trout	YE	3,500

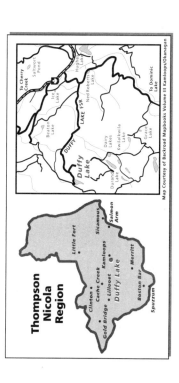

Thompson Nicola Region

Duffy Lake
Rec Site

DUFFY   LAKE   FSR

Scale

100m 0 100m 200m 300m 400m 500m

N

Access/Parking

From Little Fort on Highway #5 north of Kamloops, take the ferry across the North Thompson River. The ferry is too small to hold large trailers and RV's. Once on the east side of the river, head north on the Wildpass Road for about 4 km before the road heads sharply east. Another two kilometers and you will be at the north end of the lake.

As an alternative, longer route, you can head north on the Dunn Lake Road from Barriére. Turn right at the Esso Station and follow the main road 33 km north. You will eventually reach the south end of the lake.

Fishing

Dunn Lake is a larger 460 ha lake set below Mount Fennell and is known for its crystal clear water surrounded by scenic mountains. The lake is best trolled for the rainbow trout, dolly varden, lake trout and kokanee that range in size from 0.25 to 11 kg (0.5 to 25 lbs).

The rainbow are best taken using a gang troll (Wedding Ring or Ford Fender) or small lure (Panther Martin, Deadly Dick or Mepps). For the kokanee, a Willow Leaf and worm trolled slowly is a good bet. The lake trout like plugs and larger spoons (such as an Apex) trolled deep (30-90 ft). As a rule of thumb, the later in the summer, the deeper you should troll.

That is because earlier in the spring, you can find the fish closer to the surface but as the summer arrives, the fish retreat to the depths. For the dollies, a lure such as a Krocodile or green Flatfish is a good bet.

Fly fishing, given the clear water, is tough. Use a long light leader for best results.

Given the depth of the lake, the water does not warm significantly in the summer so fishing remains active throughout the ice-free season.

Facilities

There is an unattractive rec site at the north end of Dunn Lake offering camping and a cartop boat launch. The 2 lakeshore sites are often taken.

The Dunn Lake Resort (250-674-2344 or dunnlake@mail.wellsgray.net), located at the south end of the lake, contains 3 rustic cabins which have kerosene lights, bedding, kitchen utensils, propane camp stove and sink but no running water or toilet. A nice campground (no hookups) set in an old growth cedar stand is provided for a fee. There are boat rentals and a boat launch as well.

Other Options

Using Dunn Lake as a base, it is possible to explore a couple other lakes in the area. To the north, **Hallamore Lake** and to the south, **McTaggart Lakes** are worth visiting. Look for their descriptions in this book.

Lake Definition

Elevation: 451.2 m (1,480 ft)
Surface Area: 131 ha (923 ac)
Mean Depth: 55 m (180 ft)
Max Depth: 84 m (276 ft)
Perimeter: 12,485 m (40,950 ft)
Way Point: 51° 26' 00" Lat - N
120° 08' 00" Lon - W

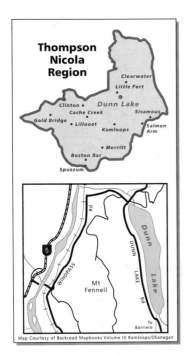

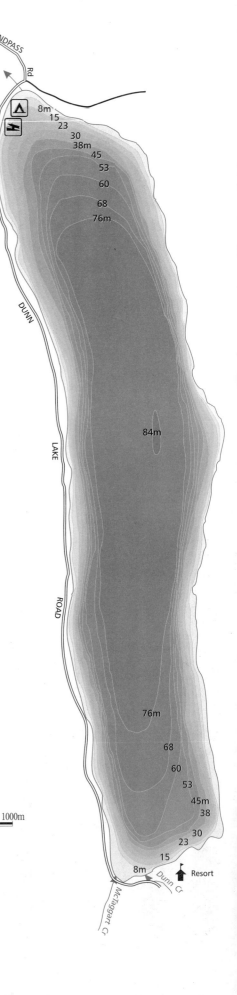

Dutch Lake

Access/Parking

Dutch lake is located in the heart of Clearwater. The town is found on Highway #5 north of Kamloops and Little Fort. Dutch Lake is set on the bank above the Clearwater River, just north of where the Clearwater River drains into the North Thompson River.

Fishing

Since Dutch Lake is located right next to the town of Clearwater, fishing pressure is heavy. Despite this, the lake is still known as a good family recreation lake, ideal for young children looking to catch their first small fish. The water drops off fairly rapidly allowing children to cast a bobber and worm from shore.

Although the lake is at 445 m (1460 ft) in elevation, it is a deep lake (maximum 41 m/135 ft) so the fishery remains active even in the heart of the summer. Trolling a gang troll (Wedding Ring and worm) or a Flatfish is a good choice. For fly fishermen, concentrate your efforts around the west side of the island located near the east end of the lake. There are some nice shoals in that area. Mayfly, shrimp or chironomid patterns are the most effective.

In the winter, the lake offers decent ice fishing using bait (worm, maggots or corn) and hook.

Facilities

The Dutch Lake Provincial Park has camping as well as a cartop boat launch. Amenities and accommodations can also be found in the town of Clearwater.

Lake Definition

Elevation:	304.8 m (999.7 ft)
Surface Area:	65 ha (161 ac)
Mean Depth:	13.6 m (44.6 ft)
Max Depth:	40.8 m (133.8 ft)
Perimeter:	3,844 m (12,608 ft)
Way Point:	51° 39' 00" Lat - N
	120° 03' 00" Lon - W

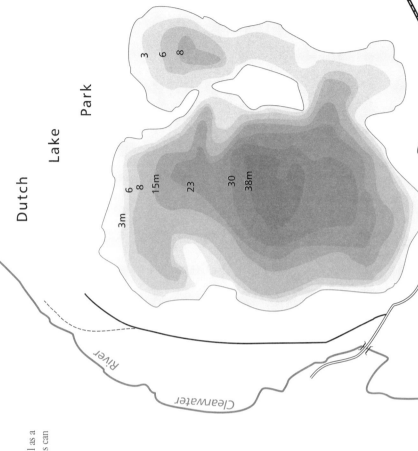

N

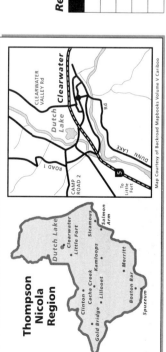

Thompson Nicola Region

Recent Fish Stocking

Year	Fish Species	Life Stage	Number
1999	rainbow trout, E brook trout	YE, FG	9,000
1998	rainbow trout, E brook trout	YE, FG	8,000
1997	rainbow trout	YE	6,000
1996	rainbow trout	YE	6,000
1995	rainbow trout	YE	7,000

East Barriére Lake

Access/Parking

East Barriére Lake is a deep, cold lake set in a narrow valley surrounded by mountains. The lake is located to the west of the Adams Lake and east of the North Thompson River Valley. There is good access to the lake so you can take a car or 2wd truck.

To access the lake, your best bet is to head to Barriére on Highway #5 north of Kamloops and then head northeast on the paved Barriére Lakes Road. After about 17.5 km you will come to a three way intersection. Take the middle branch (East Barriére Branch) and you will soon reach the west end of the lake.

If you want to explore many kilometers of dusty, windy forestry roads then try accessing the lake from the Adams Lake. Drive on the Squilax-Anglemont Road from Highway #1 until you take the Holdings Road heading to the left. This road will bring you to the Adams Lake Lumber mill and the start of the Adams Lake West logging road. Head north along the west side of Adams Lake and once you have past Skwaam Bay, take the second major logging road leading off to the left (Spapilem Creek Road). This road will rise sharply from the lakeside to East Barriére Lake, but not before you see kilometers of side roads and cutblocks. It is a good idea to bring a copy of the Backroad Mapbook Volume III Kamloops/Okanagan before trying to untangle the web of roads to find your way to East Barriére Lake.

Facilities

There is a resort and several private cabins on the lake. At the west end of the lake, there is an air strip along with a recreation site. This treeless site offers 16 camping sites, several picnic tables and a boat launch.

Fishing

East Barriére Lake does not receive the same heavy fishing pressure as the Bonaparte Plateau lakes and you should consider this lake as an option if you want to get away from the crowds. Fishing tends to be slow throughout the year but when you get a strike you are probably looking at a good size rainbow or dolly varden. Trolling a plug or spoon is the primary method of fishing the lake although fly fishermen can try some of the creek estuaries, many shoals or shallow bays. Also, trolling a fly slowly seems to work.

In terms of fly patterns to use, fly fishermen should try a chironomid pupae, mayfly nymph or damselfly nymph.

There are also some kokanee, whitefish and ling cod (burbot) in the lake.

Other Options

East Barriére Lake is the largest of a series of remote mountainous lakes. **North Barriére**, **Saskum** and **Johnson Lakes** are all described in this book. Another alternative is **South Barriére Lake**. This lake offers good fishing for rainbow in the spring and fall.

Lake Definition

Elevation:	640 m (2,100 ft)
Surface Area:	1,036 ha (2,560 ft)
Mean Depth:	47.6 m (156 ft)
Max Depth:	92 m (302 ft)
Perimeter:	25,915 m (85,000 ft)
Way Point:	51° 17' 00" Lat - N
	119° 47' 00" Lon - W

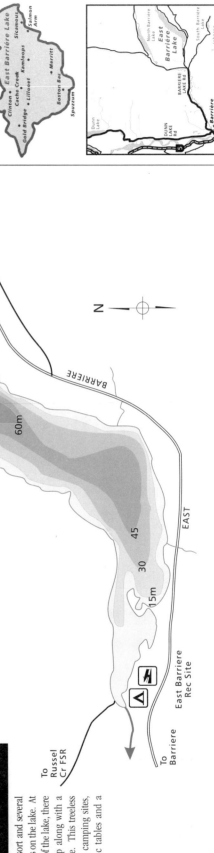

Edith Lake

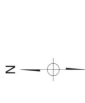

Access/Parking

Located in a prime fishing area south of Kamloops, the lake is easily accessed by 2wd road (Edith Lake Road) south of Knutsford. From Kamloops, take Highway #5A south towards Merritt. When you reach the tiny community of Knutsford, head south on the Long Lake Road. The second major road leading right from the Long Lake Road is the Edith Lake Road. A little over 3 km along that road heading southwest will bring you to the north end of the lake.

Fishing

Edith Lake is set in an open rangeland allowing easy access for shore fishermen with waders. The lake is extremely productive and grows eastern brook trout and a few rainbows quickly. For example, a fingerling stocked in the spring grows to 0.75 kg (2 lbs) by the late fall. However, the lake is very susceptible to winterkill given its maximum depth of 11.6 m (38 ft) so many of the stocked fish do not live through to their second year.

The fishing is best in the early spring and late in the fall as the water gets warm in the summer and a green plankton bloom covers the surface of the water with a green scum during most of the summer. The eastern brook trout are best caught by casting a small lure like a Deadly Dick or green Flat Fish with a worm. Bobber and worm is also a good choice.

In the fall, the eastern brook trout congregate near the shallows for breading purposes. It is at that time that the fish become extremely aggressive and fly fishing with an attractor type pattern (Doc Spratley or Wooley Bugger) can yield unbelievable results. Spincasting into the shallows is also a good choice.

The lake has four distinct narrows or bays with shallow water where there is a proliferation of insects and invertebrates. The fish are often found near these areas where the water drops off to 6 m (20 ft). Try casting at the drop-off at these locations.

Facilities

There are no developed facilities at the lake.

Other Options

The Edith Lake and Long Lake Roads give access to a few other small lakes. **McLeod** and **Nichol Lake** to the south and Goose Lake to the west can produce the odd small trout. It is recommended to visit the **Lac Le Jeune** or **Roche Lake** areas if you want a better fishing.

Lake Definition

Elevation:	1,019.8 m (3,345 ft)
Surface Area:	27 ha (66.3 ac)
Mean Depth:	5.8 m (19 ft)
Max Depth:	11.6 m (38 ft)
Perimeter:	3,862.5 m (12,672 ft)
Way Point:	50° 34' 00" Lat - N
	120° 21' 00" Lon - W

Recent Fish Stocking

Year	Fish Species	Life Stage	Number
1999	E brook trout, rainbow trout	FG	11,500
1998	E brook trout, rainbow trout	FG	11,500
1997	E brook trout, rainbow trout	FG	10,000
1996	E brook trout, rainbow trout	FG, PA	10,071
1995	E brook trout, rainbow trout	FG	10,000

N

100m   0   100m   200m   300m   400m   500m

Scale

Gannett Lake

Access/Parking

Gannett Lake is found in a logged out valley to the northeast of Adams Lake. A thin leave strip of trees surrounds the lake.

From the Trans Canada Highway 5.5 km northeast of Chase, take the Squilax-Anglemont Road leading north. This paved road immediately crosses a bridge over the Shuswap Lake and then heads north. Soon you will have to turn left at the first major intersection and follow the paved Holdings Road that winds gently along the western banks of the Adams River to the south end of the lake. Continue northward along the Holdings Road to the mill and from there, an excellent, well graded but windy mainhaul logging road will bring you to the north end of the Adams Lake.

The Gannett Lake Forest Service Road is a major logging road heading to the left at 3.5 km on the Adams Lake East Road. This logging road is in good shape and brings you up into the Gannett Creek drainage from the Adams Lake. Shortly after passing Telfer Lake, you will see a sign and road leading to Gannett Lake.

Facilities

There is a small forest service rec site on the north end of the lake near the largest bay. The road into the rec site is a little narrow and best suited for trucks. A cartop boat launch is found at the rec site.

Other Options

Look for the **Telfer Lake** description in this book.

Lake Definition

Elevation:	1,021.1 m (3,350 ft)
Surface Area:	77.6 ha (192 ac)
Mean Depth:	8.5 m (27.9 ft)
Max Depth:	27 m (88.6 ft)
Perimeter:	5,360 m (17,585 ft)
Way Point:	51° 28' 00" Lat - N
	119° 21' 00" Lon - W

Fishing

Gannett Lake is not considered the best fishing lake in the area but it does offer good fishing for rainbow trout that can reach 1 kg (average 20-25 cm/8-10"). The lake is best fly fished or in the spring and fall. Spincasting or flyfishing from shores is fairly hard given the expansive shallows and weeds so you should use a float tube or boat.

The lake has many bays, shallows and weed beds idea for insect and invertebrate growth. Fly fishermen should pick one of those areas and try matching the insect hatch of the season. Trolling is best performed in the middle of the two main bodies of water where the water is deepest.

The lake is deep enough (27 m/87 ft) that the water does not warm significantly in the summer to affect fishing.

Gannett Lake Recreation Site

Gannett Mnt

Thompson Nicola Region

Clearwater
Little Fort
Gannett Lake
Sicamous
Salmon Arm
Kamloops
Clinton
Cache Creek
Lillooet
Merritt
Gold Bridge
Boston Bar
Spuzzum

Cannett Lake
Telfer Lake
GANNETT EAST FSR
ADAMS
Adams Lake
To Chase

Map Courtesy of Backroad Mapbook Volume: III Kamloops/Okanagan

N

FSR

LAKE

GANNETT

Gannett Cr

Scale
100m   0   100m   200m   300m   400m   500m

Glimpse Lake

Access/Parking

Glimpse Lake is found north of Douglas Lake and east of Nicola Lake in cattle country. To reach the lake, begin on Highway 5A from either Kamloops or Merritt and near the north end of Nicola Lake, you will find the Douglas Lake Road. Drive east on the road and at the first major intersection, take the Lauder Road heading northeast. That road will take you directly to the south end of Glimpse Lake.

An alternative route is to take the Peterhope Road, which begins 3 km south of Stump Lake on Highway #5A. This road first leads to Peterhope Lake and then at the 17.5 km mark, head south and you will be at Glimpse Lake in less then a kilometer.

Lake Definition

Elevation: 1,219 m (4,000 ft)
Surface Area: 95 ha (235 ac)
Mean Depth: 21 m (70 ft)
Max Depth: 7,148.5 m (23,453 ft)
Perimeter: 50° 15' 00" Lat - N
Way Point: 120° 17' 00" Lon - W

Fishing

The fishing season for rainbow to 1 kg (2 lbs) begins at Glimpse Lake in early May and runs until mid-July when the summer doldrums set in. By late September, the fishing picks up again until the ice comes in November.

Glimpse Lake has many weed beds particularly at the east end of the lake. Also, the shoreline of the lake is covered with reeds making it an ideal location to cast a damselfly (green colour is best) or a dragonfly nymph. The clear water of the lake makes presentation very important. A sedge pattern in the early summer during the hatch is also a good choice.

The lake is tough to troll unless you focus around the deep part near the west end of the lake. Spincasters do well with a small spinner (Mepps, Blue Fox or Panther Martin) cast towards the reeds.

An electric motor only restriction is in effect at the lake.

Facilities

The lake has a rec site with a cartop boat launch and basic camping sites. The lake also has a resort and several private properties on it.

Other Options

If the fish are not biting at Glimpse Lake, try Blue Lake or Little Blue Lake to the northeast:

Blue Lake is located northeast of Glimpse Lake off the Lauder Road (rough 2wd access). The lake is 12 ha in size and located at 1220 m (4000 ft) in elevation. It is renowned for having larger rainbow (to 2+ kg/5 lbs) but is notoriously difficult to fish.

Little Blue Lake offers surprisingly good fishing for rainbow trout that can grow to 1.5 kg in size probably because the 4wd access discourages fishermen. The 7 ha lake is at 1270 m (4170 ft) in elevation and is stocked with rainbow.

Recent Fish Stocking

Year	Fish Species	Life Stage	Number
1999	rainbow trout	YE	10,000
1998	rainbow trout	YE	10,000
1997	rainbow trout	YE	12,000
1996	rainbow trout	YE	12,000
1995	rainbow trout	YE	15,000

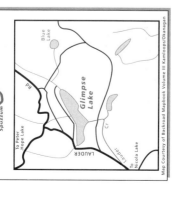

Thompson Nicola Region

Map Courtesy of Backroad Mapbook Volume III Kamloops/Okanagan

Gorman Lake

Thompson Nicola Region

N

To Allan and Scott Lake

Gorman Lake Rec Site

GORMAN LAKE

FSR

To Hwy 5

Scale

Access/Parking

Gorman Lake is located on the Bonaparte Plateau to the west of the North Thompson River Valley. To reach the lake, head north from Kamloops on Highway #5 and look for the Westsyde Road just after the North Thompson River bridge near Barriére. Climb 4.5 km from Highway #5 on the Westsyde Road to the Gorman Lake Forest Service Road junction. This logging road continues through the valley. After 15.5 km, you will reach the lake. The Gorman Lake Road is one of the main arteries leading into the Bonaparte Plateau and can be travelled by RV's and vehicles with trailers.

Fishing

Gorman Lake, despite its easy access and muddy shoreline, offers fairly good fishing for rainbow trout that can reach 1 kg (2 lbs) in size. Bait fishing, spincasting and fly fishing are the mainstays of the lake. The fishery remains active throughout the ice-free season.

For fly fishermen, casting or slowly trolling a leech patterns is effective throughout the year. Damselfly nymph in June and September are dynamite at times; as is a chironomid pupae in early spring and late fall retrieved slowly from the depths of the lake. The sedge hatch offers good dry fly fishing in late June-early July.

The swampy lake has two distinctive deep spots, one near the northwest end of the lake and one in the middle. Nice shoals exist at both the northwest and southeast ends of the lake. Try casting around the shoals and at the drop-offs.

Facilities

Gorman Lake Rec Site has 5 functional camping units in a grassy area next to the lake. The edge of the lake is extremely swampy making launching a boat quite difficult.

Other Options

The Bonaparte Plateau offers litterally hundreds of lakes to sample. Continuing west, you have the option of accessing either **Allan Lake** or **Scot Lake**.

Allan Lake is better described at the beginning of this book.
Scot Lake is known to produce rainbow in the spring and fall. There is also a rec site with a boat launch on the lake.

Lake Definition

Elevation: 1,135 m (4,051 ft)
Surface Area: 20 ha (49.4 ft)
Mean Depth: 3.8 m (12.4 ft)
Max Depth: 10 m (34 ft)
Perimeter: 2,432.3 m (7,980 ft)
Way Point: 51° 13' 00" Lat - N
120° 15' 00" Lon - W

Recent Fish Stocking

Year	Fish Species	Life Stage	Number
1998	rainbow trout	FF	4,000
1997	rainbow trout	FF	4,000
1996	rainbow trout	FF	4,000
1995	rainbow trout	FF	4,000

Hallamore Lake

Axel Creek

Axel Cr

ROAD

LAKE

DUNN

To McCarthy Lake and Clearwater

To Dunn lake

6m 9 12 15m 18 21

Lake Definition

Elevation:	915 m (3,000 ft)
Surface Area:	24 ha (59 ac)
Mean Depth:	13.4 m (44 ft)
Max Depth:	23 m (74 ft)
Perimeter:	2,453.7 m (8,050 ft)
Way Point:	51° 30' 00" Lat - N
	120° 08' 00" Lon - W

Access/Parking

Hallamore Lake is a 24 ha lake located to the north of Dunn Lake near the Boulder Creek Indian Reserve. The Queen Bess Mine is also situated near the north end of the lake.

From Little Fort on Highway #5 north of Kamloops, take the ferry across the North Thompson River. Once on the east side of the river, head north on the Wildpass Road for about 4 km before the road heads sharply east. Another two kilometers and you will be at the north end of Dunn Lake. Turn north on the Dunn Lake Road and Hallamore Lake is a short distance away.

As an alternative, longer route, you can head north on the Dunn Lake Road from Barriére. Turn right at the Esso Station and follow the main road north. You will eventually reach the south end of Dunn Lake. Continue north past Dunn Lake to Hallamore Lake.

Fishing

Hallamore Lake is an inviting lake with drop-offs circling the entire lake. The lake is 23 m (74 ft) deep in the middle so winterkill is not a real problem and the water does not warm enough to make the summer doldrums a severe problem. It contains rainbow to 1.5 kg (2-3 lbs) although the average fish tends to be quite small.

Trolling a gang troll (Willow Leaf or Ford Fender) with a worm is a good bet as is trolling a fly (Leech, Doc Spratley or Carey Special) or small lure (Mepps, Kamlooper or Panther Martin).

Fly fishermen and spincasters can do well focusing at the Axel Creek estuary at the north end of the lake or by trying the outflow area at the south end. The usual hatches common to other lakes in the region occur here.

Facilities

There is an undeveloped camping area at the lake. It is also possible to launch small boats at the lake.

Other Options

Hallamore Lake is found north of the popular **Dunn Lake**, which is found earlier in this book. **McCarthy Lake** is a small lake found even further north. Fly fishing or spin casting can produce small rainbow.

N

Scale

100m 0 100m 200m 300m 400m 500m

Thompson Nicola Region

Hallamore Lake
Clearwater
Little Fort
Sicamous
Salmon Arm
Clinton
Cache Creek
Kamloops
Gold Bridge
Lillooet
Merritt
Boston Bar
Spuzzum

Hallamore Lake
Dunn Lake
DUNN LAKE Rd
To Clearwater
Thompson
NORTH THOMPSON
WINDPASS Rd
To Kamloops
Little Fort

Map Courtesy of Backroad Mapbook Volume V Cariboo

Hammer Lake

Access/Parking

Hammer Lake gets its name from the shape of the lake. The "handle" part of the lake is at the south end of the lake and is 9.8 m (32 ft) deep. The "head" of the lake is located to the north end and is only 4.5 m (15 ft) deep.

Hammer Lake is located southwest of Bonaparte Lake. To access the lake, your best bet is to follow the North Bonaparte Road from either Highway 24 or 97. Continue to the Rayfield River and look for the Egan-Bonaparte Forest Service Road. Follow that road south to Hammer Lake. If you reach Bonaparte Lake, you have gone too far.

Despite the long haul on logging roads, RV's and trailers can access the lake. A copy of the Backroad Mapbook for the Kamloops/Okanagan will definitely help in locating the many lakes on the Bonaparte Plateau.

Facilities

The Hammer Lake Rec Site is located in a treeless area at the north end of the lake. The 9 campsites include 6 prime lakeside sites. There is also a cartop boat launch.

Fishing

Hammer Lake is a good fly fishing and spincasting lake for rainbow in the 1-2 kg (2-5 lbs) category. Given the depth of the lake, trolling is limited to surface flies or lures unless you like to catch "weed trout". The lake is also lined with reeds.

After ice-off in early May, the lake offers a series of good chironomid hatches right into early June. Use a #10-14 pupae pattern sunk to the bottom and retrieved very slowly. Olive, black, maroon and brown colours all work.

Beginning in late June, cast a damselfly or dragonfly nymph into the reeds and hang on. Some days the fly fishing can be absolutely unbelievable.

For the dry fly fishermen, a good sedge hatch occurs in late June and into early July. Focus on the late evening as that is when the hatch is at its peak and the fish are often jumping feverishly. Green coloured patterns are most consistent producers.

By summer, the water warms and the summer doldrums set in. Fishing becomes incredibly slow except for the odd bite late in the evening or early in the morning. By late fall, good insect hatches start occurring again and fishing picks up.

An electric motor only restriction applies.

Other Options

While in the area, check out **Scot Lake** to the west.

Lake Definition

Elevation:	1,311 m (4,300 ft)
Surface Area:	68.4 ha (169 ac)
Mean Depth:	3.4 m (11 ft)
Max Depth:	9.8 m (32 ft)
Perimeter:	5,647 m (18,480 ft)
Way Point:	51° 15' 00" Lat - N
	120° 45' 00" Lon - W

Recent Fish Stocking

Year	Fish Species	Life Stage	Number
1999	rainbow trout	YE	10,000
1997	rainbow trout	FF	10,000
1996	rainbow trout	FF	9,847
1995	rainbow trout	FF	10,000

Thompson Nicola Region

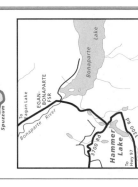

Map Courtesy of Backroad Mapbook Volume III Kamloops/Okanagan

Harbour Lake

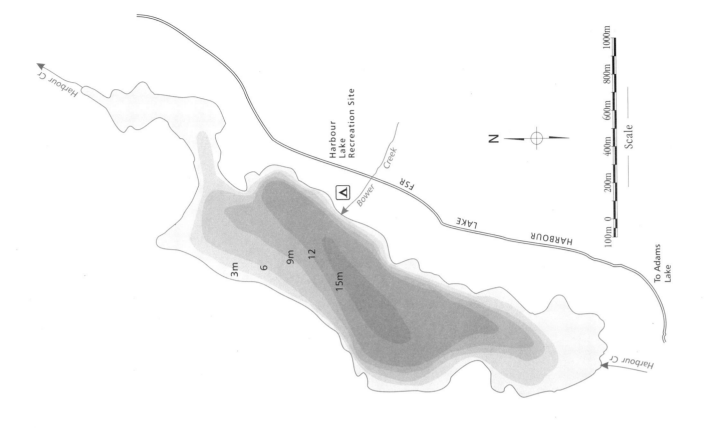

Access/Parking

Harbour Lake is located northeast of the Adams Lake in a remote area of B.C.

From the Trans Canada Highway 5.5 km northeast of Chase, take the Squilax-Anglemont Road leading north. This paved road immediately crosses a bridge over the Shuswap Lake and then heads north. Soon you will have to turn left at the first major intersection and follow the paved Holdings Road that winds gently along the western banks of the Adams River to the south end of the lake. Continue northward along the Holdings Road to the mill and from there, an excellent, well graded but windy mainhaul logging road will bring you to the north end of the Adams Lake.

Once at the north end of the Adams Lake, continue on the Harbour Lake Forest Service Road, which follows the Adams River and you will eventually reach the lake.

A truck is highly recommended.

Fishing

Harbour Lake is a 54 ha lake, which does not receive a lot of fishing pressure. Therefore, it produces well for small rainbow up to 1 kg (2-3 lbs) in size. The north and south ends of the lake have some nice shallows near the inflow and outflow creeks ideal for spincasting and fly fishing. Trollers can work the drop-offs along the western and eastern shores of the lake.

The lake can be fished as early as mid-May. The summer doldrums are not much of a problem as the lake is fairly deep (maximum 18.3 m/60 ft). By early November, the ice is back on the lake.

Facilities

There is a small rustic campsite next to the road and Bower Creek. Throw a bobber and worm at the creek mouth and you may get lucky.

A cartop boat launch is at the lake.

Other Options

While in this remote area, be sure time to explore some of the other lakes in the area. **Mica Lake** is a small lake found west of Harbour Lake. **Telfer**, **Gannett** and **Tsikwustum Lakes** are found in the drainages to the south.

For a completely different experience, why not try **Adams Lake**. This large lake contains rainbow trout which average 3kg (8 lbs). There are also some large lake trout and dolly varden. Trolling is by far the most productive method of fishing, especially in the spring and fall. In the summer kokanee fishing can be good.

Lake Definition

Elevation: 857 m (2,810 ft)
Surface Area: 54.2 ha (134 ac)
Mean Depth: 7.7 m (25.2 ft)
Max Depth: 18.3 m (60 ft)
Perimeter: 5,276.2 m (17,310 ft)
Way Point: 51° 33' 00" Lat - N
119° 11' 00" Lon - W

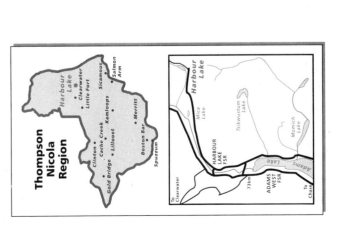

Harper Lake

Access/Parking

Harper Lake is located south of Chase on the hill above the South Thompson River. A 2wd road (Harper lake Road) leading sharply uphill from Highway #1 accesses the lake. To find the Harper Lake Road, simply drive south from Chase to the tiny community of Shuswap where the road begins.

Access is fairly good but a truck is certainly a benefit.

Facilities

There is a rec site found on the western shores of Harper Lake, which offers camping and a cartop boat launch.

Other Options

Niskonlith and **Little Shuswap** Lakes are found north of Harper Lake. Both of these lakes are better described in this book.

Lake Definition

Elevation:	671 m (2,200 ft)
Surface Area:	28 ha (70.3 ft)
Mean Depth:	12 m (39.6 ft)
Max Depth:	23 m (75 ft)
Perimeter:	1,420.4 m (9,660 ft)
Way Point:	50° 44' 00" Lat - N
	119° 43' 00" Lon - W

Fishing

Harper Lake is a tea-coloured lake which offers good fishing for rainbow which offers good fishing for rainbow which reach 2 kg (4-5 lbs). The lake is nutrient rich with a lot of insects and aquatic vertebrae so the fish grow rapidly.

The lake is 23 m (75 ft) deep and has nice drop-offs along its entire shoreline. The best shoals are located at the northeast and southwest ends of the lake.

Ice-off occurs in late April so the lake can be fished most of May through to late June with good success. Unfortunately, the summer doldrums soon hit the lake beginning in early July and extends into September. By October, the lake is producing again.

The preferred method of fishing is by artificial fly as there is a bait ban, single hook restriction and ice fishing ban at the lake. Fly fishermen should definitely visit the lake in June when the caddisfly hatch is in full swing. A pupae imitation is very effective. At other times of the year, a leech, shrimp or dragonfly pattern are good producers.

Be forewarned the fish are very picky about your presentation so fishing can be frustrating for novice casters.

Recent Fish Stocking

Year	Fish Species	Life Stage	Number
1999	rainbow trout	YE	4,000
1998	rainbow trout	YE	4,000
1997	rainbow trout	YE	4,000
1996	rainbow trout	YE	4,000
1995	rainbow trout	YE	4,000

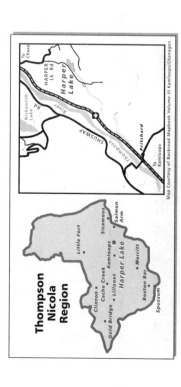

Thompson Nicola Region

Map Courtesy of Backroad Mapbook Volume III Kamloops/Okanagan

Hatheume Lake

Access/Parking

There is very good access to Hatheume Lake allowing even an RV or car to approach the lake.

The designers of the Okanagan Connector, in their wisdom, have limited access to the logging roads of the area to the Sunset Exit. Therefore, you must exit the Okanagan Connector at the Sunset Exit, drive to the south of the connector and then travel 6 km east right beside the highway. At the 6 km mark, a major intersection will appear. Travel a very short distance south on the Sunset Lake Forest Service Road and you will see the Bear Creek Forest Service Road heading off to the left. Take that road under the Okanagan Connector and you are on your way to the lake.

While travelling northeast on the Bear Creek Forest Service Road, avoid taking the road to Pennask Lake and you will soon see the well signed exit to Hatheume Lake. Simply follow the signs all the way to the lake from the Sunset Exit.

Fishing

Hatheume Lake has seen a dramatic increase in fishing success over the last few years. This is because the lake is now heavily regulated as a quality fishery. There is a one trout limit, an ice-fishing ban, a barbless hook restriction, an engine size restriction (no motors over 10 hp) and an artificial fly only requirement.

The lake is only 12 m (40 ft) deep and so it tends to warm in the summer months creating a slow down in the fishing. The lake has some nice shoals particularly at the northwest and southeast ends of the lake. The inflow creek at the southeast end of the lake and the outflow at the north end of the lake are two very inviting locations to fish.

Rainbow in the 1.5 kg (3–4 lb) range are now being caught on a consistent basis. Beginning after the ice leaves in mid-May, a series of good spring chironomid hatches occur until early June. Brown and black pupae patterns sunk to the bottom and retrieved very slowly is the best way to fish the hatch. In late June-early July, a sedge hatch makes dry fly fishing a real pleasure. Damselfly, dragonfly and mayfly patterns work with varying success over the spring and into the fall.

Facilities

At the southeast corner of the lake, you will find the **Hatheume Lake Rec Site**. The rec site has 20, treed camping site together with pit toilets, picnic tables and a cartop boat launch. If you are interested in more luxurious surroundings, the Hatheume Resort is the place for you. It use to be a run down resort but Triple 8 Development has done an excellent job of developing the resort by selling individual cabins to private owners and extensively upgrading the cabins. Also, several Lindel Homes were added to the resort.

Other Options

Hatheume Lake is one of several lakes located north of the Okanagan Connector (Hwy 97c). Other options include **Ellen**, **Pinnacle**, **Peterson** and **Pennask Lake**. Rainbow are the predominant speicies of the region. Fishing with a fly or spin casting is best in the spring and fall.

Lake Definition

Elevation:	1,395 m (4,576 ft)
Surface Area:	134 ha (331 ac)
Mean Depth:	5.4 m (17.7 ft)
Max Depth:	12 m (39.4 ft)
Perimeter:	5,860 m (19,220 ft)
Way Point:	49° 49' 00" Lat - N 120° 03' 00" Lon - W

Recent Fish Stocking

Year	Fish Species	Life Stage	Number
1999	rainbow trout	YE, FG	3,500
1998	rainbow trout	YE, FG	3,500
1997	rainbow trout	YE	2,000
1996	rainbow trout	YE	2,000
1995	rainbow trout	YE	2,000

N

Hatheume Lake South Rec Site

resort
dam

Scale

100m 0   200m   400m   600m

To Bear Creek Rd

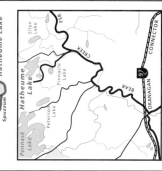

Thompson Nicola Region

Little Fort
Sicamous
Salmon Arm
Clinton
Cache Creek
Kamloops
Gold Bridge
Lillooet
Merritt
Boston Bar
Spuzzum
Hatheume Lake

Ellen Lake
FSR
Hatheume Lake
Peterson Lake
Pinnacle Lake
Pennask Lake
BEAR CREEK
OKANAGAN CONNECTOR
97

Map Courtesy of Backroad Mapbook Volume III Kamloops/Okanagan

Heffley Lake

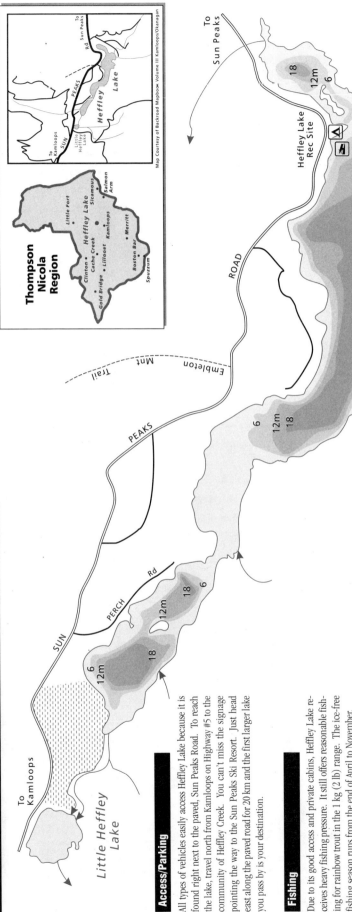

Map Courtesy of Backroad Mapbook Volume III Kamloops/Okanagan

Thompson Nicola Region

Access/Parking

All types of vehicles easily access Heffley Lake because it is found right next to the paved, Sun Peaks Road. To reach the lake, travel north from Kamloops on Highway #5 to the community of Heffley Creek. You can't miss the signage pointing the way to the Sun Peaks Ski Resort. Just head east along the paved road for 20 km and the first larger lake you pass by is your destination.

Fishing

Due to its good access and private cabins, Heffley Lake receives heavy fishing pressure. It still offers reasonable fishing for rainbow trout in the 1 kg (2 lb) range. The ice-free fishing season runs from the end of April to November.

Although trolling is popular, fly fishing should not be ruled out. Fly fishermen should try the shoals at the west end of the lake during the spring damselfly, chironomid or mayfly hatch. This is because there are some excellent weed beds great for insects and hiding rainbow. At the east end of the lake, you will find the inlet creek and the spawning channel. You can do well fishing near the deep pocket northeast of the small island. Also, the numerous bays and shallow areas on the main body of water offer many choice locations to cast a fly. Fly patterns of choice are a damselfly or dragonfly nymph, shrimp imitations, Doc Spratley, chironomid papa and bloodworm, mayfly and Leeches.

Spincasting a small lure (Flatfish, Mepps, Blue Fox or Kamlooper) around the drop-offs or near the inflow and outflow creeks can be productive.

The lake warms in the summer months forcing the fish to the depths of the lakes. At this time, trolling with a Willow Leaf and worm, Flatfish or Apex is recommended. The lake begins to cool in late September to October. At that time, fly fishing and spincasting the shoals and drop-offs becomes productive again. In the winter months, ice fishing with bait and a hook is effective.

Facilities

Heffley Lake has two resorts. The Heffley Lake Fishing Resort (250-578-7251 or heffleylake@bc.sympatico.ca) is on the south side of the lake and offers some rustic cabins from May to October. Lakeshore camp sites (with hook-ups), boat rentals and hot showers are other features of the resort.

The Hitch' N Reel Family Resort also offers cozy lakeshore cabins at a reasonable rate together with camping sites (partial and full hook-ups). A central washroom with hot showers and flush toilets, boat rentals, convenience store and restaurant are some of the other amenities of the resort.

There is also a heavily used rec site, which has a cartop boat launch as well as a few camping spots. The main grassy area is often full but there is a seperate, treed peninsula to the right.

Other Options

Little Heffley Lake also produces stocked rainbow trout. This 7 ha lake is best fished by fly or spin casting. The damselfly and mayfly hatches are particularly productive.

Lake Definition

Elevation:	943.3 m (3,095 ft)
Surface Area:	202.8 ha (550 ac)
Mean Depth:	10.9 m (36 ft)
Max Depth:	23.4 m (77 ft)
Perimeter:	14,967.1 m (49,104 ft)
Way Point:	50° 50' 00" Lat - N
	120° 04' 00" Lon - W

Recent Fish Stocking

Year	Fish Species	Life Stage	Number
1999	rainbow trout	YE	12,000
1998	rainbow trout	YE	12,000
1997	rainbow trout	YE	12,000
1996	rainbow trout	YE	12,000
1995	rainbow trout	YE	12,000

Hoopatatkwa Lake

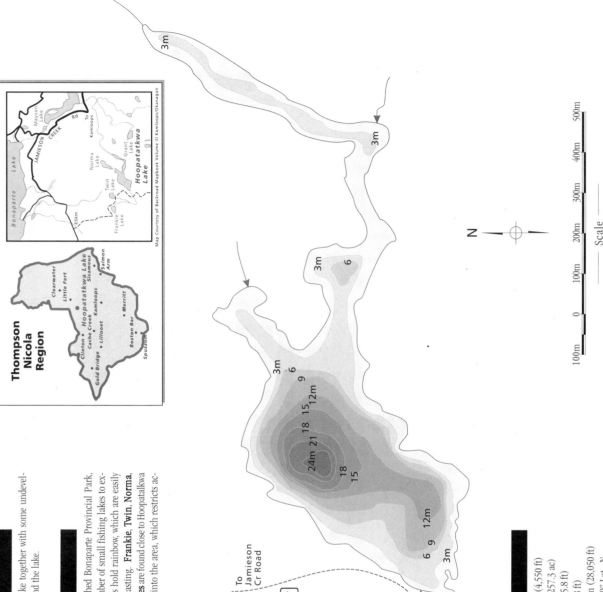

Map Courtesy of Backroad Mapbook Volume III Kamloops/Okanagan

Access/Parking

Hoopatatkwa Lake is found at the north end of Bonaparte Provincial Park. There is no road access into the lake so you will have to make a long hike from the 65 km marker on the Jamieson Creek Road or fly in to the lake.

To find the trailhead, is no easy task either. Take the Westsyde Road north of Kamloops until you reach the Jamieson Creek Road heading off to the left. The junction is on the west bank of the North Thompson River north of the Lac Du Bois Grasslands Provincial Park.

Head north on the Jamieson Creek Road avoiding the temptation to veer off the main road on one of the many logging roads leading from the Jamieson Creek Road. By the time you reach the trailhead after 65 km of gravel road you probably won't mind stretching your legs with a good walk.

Fishing

Hoopatatkwa Lake, due to its remote access, offers good fishing for rainbow trout to 2 kg (5 lbs) by fly fishing, bait fishing or spincasting.

The lake has a deep hole (27 m/88 ft) right in the middle of the lake. Also, some inviting drop-offs are located at the south and north end of the main water body. A good shoal area extends to the east and west of the deep hole. The narrow bay to the east of the main body is not worth fishing as it is only 3 m (10 ft) deep.

For dry fly fishermen, getting to the lake in late June or early July will reward you with a good sedge hatch. Damselfly, mayfly nymph and chironomid pupae patterns also work depending on the hatch. Just before dusk is a particularly good time to fish on this lake.

In the summer, the fish retreat to the deep hole. Fishing slows in the summer months but that does not rule out using a sinking line with a nymph pattern or Doc Spratley fished deep. Also, bait fishing into the depths of the lake at that time of year can be effective.

By the early fall, the hatches are back into full swing and fishing the shoals and drop-offs is effective again.

Facilities

There is a resort at the lake together with some undeveloped camping areas around the lake.

Other Options

Within the newly established Bonaparte Provincial Park, there is an unlimited number of small fishing lakes to explore. Many of these lakes hold rainbow, which are easily taken on a fly or by spin casting. **Frankie, Twin, Norma, Martha** and **Dumbell Lakes** are found close to Hoopatatkwa Lake. There are no roads into the area, which restricts access to foot or canoe.

Lake Definition

Elevation:	1,387 m (4,550 ft)
Surface Area:	104 ha (257.3 ac)
Mean Depth:	7.9 m (25.8 ft)
Max Depth:	27 m (88 ft)
Perimeter:	8,549.7 m (28,050 ft)
Way Point:	51° 12' 00" Lat - N
	120° 28' 00" Lon - W

Hyas Lake & Area

Access/Parking

This series of small mountain lakes are accessed by the Hyas Lake Road, a rough logging road best left to a high clearance vehicle.

To reach the lakes, take the Paul Lake Road turnoff after crossing the South Thompson River Bridge on Highway #5 heading north. The Paul Lake Road heads east towards Paul Lake but before you reach the lake, take the Pinantan-Pritchard Road to the left. That road represents the last major intersection before Paul Lake. Once on the Pinantan-Pritchard Road, pass by Pinantan Lake and then, 5km later, you will find a major logging road heading north called the Hyas Lake Road. Follow that road to its end and you will reach Pemberton and Hyas Lakes. Hadlow Lake involves a hike from Hyas Lake.

Facilities

The Hyas Lake Resort (1-250-319-1404 or www.oppub.com) offers rustic accommodation at a reasonable price from May to September. There are 4 cedar, lakeshore cabins with wood heaters, kitchen utensils, propane lighting, private outhouse and propane stoves. The resort also has some unserviced campsites and rents rowboats.

A rec site is located next to the Hyas Lake Resort at the south end of the lake. The rec site has 7 campsites together with a cartop boat launch.

Pemberton Lake has a 4 vehicle unit rec site together with a cartop boat launch.

Fishing

At **Hyas Lake** fishing begins in early May and runs until November. Although, fishing tails off in the summer months to some extent the elevation and the depth ensures that the water does not warm significantly in the summer.

The fishing at Hyas Lake tends to be slow. The rainbow are usually in the 0.5-1 kg (1-2.5 lb) range although an 3.5 kg (8 lbs) rainbow was caught in September, 1997. Since Hyas Lake has deep clear water, trolling is the primary fishing method. In particular, try trolling a leech pattern or a gang troll along the prominent drop-offs for best success.

For the fly fishermen, the lake has a steep shoreline on the east and west sides, which can be sampled. Nice shoals are located near the north and south ends of the lake. The fringes of several deep pockets of water are also a focus area for fly fishing. The lake offers some very rewarding insect hatches. Leech, damselfly nymph, chironomid pupae, sedge or dragonfly nymph patterns are your best bet.

Hadlow Lake is a good option if the crowds are getting too much to handle or the fish are not biting at Hyas Lake. The lake contains rainbow that can reach 1 kg (2-3 lbs) but are generally pan size. The lake is best fished by casting a lure and worm (Deadly Dick, Blue Fox or Panther Martin) or by fly fishing with a damselfly or sedge imitation. The sedge hatch in the spring is the best time to fly fish.

The lake is stocked periodically given the fact that it is only 5.5 m (18 ft) deep and winterkill is a real problem. The summer doldrums are also very prominent at the lake.

Pemberton Lake provides fairly good fishing for rainbow that can reach 1.5 kg (2-3 lbs) but are usually quite small. Extensive weedbeds line the lake offering good insect and aquatic vertebrae rearing grounds and good fish habitat. The lake is best fly fished using a damselfly or dragonfly nymph cast near the weeds. Shrimp imitations and leech patterns also work well.

Some fishermen troll the lake using a gang troll (Willow Leaf and worm) but the depth and size of the lake requires careful maneuvering. Trolling a small lure or spinner

(Flatfish, Blue Fox, Deadly Dick or Mepps) or a fly (Leech or Doc Spratley) can also be productive.

It is best to fish the lake beginning in mid-May until early July and again in late September to late October. In the summer, the lake is subject to drawdown for irrigation purposes. The water warms significantly at that time of year.

Note: There is an ice fishing ban on these lakes

Lake Definition (Hyas Lake)

Elevation: 1,238 m (4,060 ft)
Surface Area: 64 ha (158 ac)
Mean Depth: 8.2 m (27 ft)
Max Depth: 21.9 ft (72 ft)
Way Point: 50° 48' 00" Lat - N
119° 58' 00" Lon - W

Lake Definition (Pemberton Lk)

Elevation: 1,232 m (4,040 ft)
Surface Area: 12.5 ha (31 ac)
Mean Depth: 5.2 m (17 ft)
Max Depth: 13.7 m (45 ft)
Perimeter: 2,127.5 m (6,980 ft)

Recent Fish Stocking (Hadlow Lake)

Year	Fish Species	Life Stage	Number
1997	rainbow trout	FF	2,000
1995	rainbow trout	FF	2,000

Recent Fish Stocking (Hyas Lake)

Year	Fish Species	Life Stage	Number
1998	rainbow trout	FF	7,000
1997	rainbow trout	FF	6,000

Recent Fish Stocking (Pemberton Lake)

Year	Fish Species	Life Stage	Number
1997	rainbow trout	FR	10,000
1996	rainbow trout	FF	1,500

Hadlow Lake

Hyas Lake

Pemberton Lake

Hyas Lake Rec Site

Pemberton Lake Rec Site

N

Scale
200m 0 200m 400m 600m

Thompson Nicola Region

Little Fort
Clinton
Cache Creek · Sicamous
Salmon Arm
Gold Bridge · Lillooet · Kamloops
Boston Bar · Merritt
Spuzzum

Eileen Lake FSR
Eileen Lake
Hadlow Lake
Hyas Lake
Pemberton Lake
PAUL Cr FSR
HYAS LAKE Rd
Andy Lake
To Paul Lake & Kamloops
Pinantan Lake

Map Courtesy of Backroad Mapbook Volume III Kamloops/Okanagan

Island Lake

Access/Parking

Island Lake is one of 13 lakes located in an area north of the Elkhart Exit on the Okanagan Connector (Highway 97C). After exiting the highway, head north on the Elkhart Road and hang a right at the north end of Bob's Lake. Island Lake will soon appear on the left side of the road within a few hundred meters followed by Paradise Lake on the right side.

Fishing

Good fishing at Island Lake begins mid-May when the ice leaves the 34 ha lake. Island Lake is stocked with plentiful small rainbow (under 0.5 kg/1 lb).

The lake has a large island towards the southwest end which has nice shoals covered with a thick weed bed. The perimeter of the clear lake also has productive shoals with lots of vegetation ideal for insect growth. The fish are often seen cruising the shallows in the early spring and late fall.

Island Lake is only 8 m (26 ft) deep and so it suffers occasional winterkill. A deep pocket is located in the middle of the lake and another one is just southwest of the island. In the summer, the fishing falls off but you may wish to cast along the fringes of these two deep potholes.

There are good chironomid, caddisfly and mayfly hatches. Belly boats are a must at the lake.

Facilities

There is a rec site with a cartop boat launch and 5 camping units located on the north end of the lake. It can be busy during the summer months.

Other Options

Nearby **Paradise Lake** is described later in this book. Other descent lakes in the area include **Johns Lake**, **Skunk Lake**, **Bob's Lake**, **Elkhart Lake**, **Boot Lake** and **Reservoir Lake**. These small high elevation lakes offer small rainbow that are readily taken on a fly or by spin casting.

Lake Definition

Elevation:	1,524 m (4,999 ft)
Surface Area:	34.1 ha (84.2 ac)
Mean Depth:	4 m (13 ft)
Max Depth:	8 m (26 ft)
Way Point:	51° 53' 00" Lat - N
	121° 49' 00" Lon - W

Recent Fish Stocking

Year	Fish Species	Life Stage	Number
1998	rainbow trout	FF	4,000
1997	rainbow trout	FF	2,000

N

Island Lake
Rec Site

3

5m

3

3

5m

Scale

100m   0   100m   200m

To Elkhart Rd

To Paradise Lake

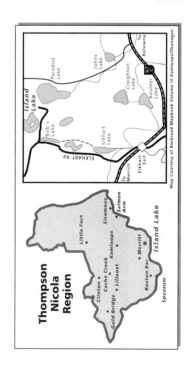

Thompson Nicola Region

Map Courtesy of Backroad Mapbook Volume III Kamloops/Okanagan

Isobel Lake

Access/Parking

Isobel Lake is located just north of the Lac Du Bois Grasslands Provincial Park, which, in turn, is found north of Kamloops and west of the North Thompson River. The lake can be reached by one of two ways. Take the Lac Du Bois Road north from Kamloops to the 15 km mark. Hang a right and you will soon pass by McQueen Lake and Griffin Lake. Within a few hundred meters of Griffin Lake, the access road to Isobel Lake leads north. The lake is 2 km away.

The second route is to head north on the Westsyde Road from Kamloops and before leaving the Lac Du Bois Grasslands Provincial Park, turn on the Long Lake Road. Take the first right heading north to access the McQueen Lake Forest Service Road. Just before Griffen Lake, the access road to Isobel Lake heads north.

Fishing

Isobel Lake is unique because it has a good population of brook trout. The fishery is maintained by an annual stocking program and the fish reach 1-1.5 kg (2-4 lbs) but tend to be pan size.

Brook trout are notoriously hard to catch with a fly except in the fall around spawning season. Casting an attractor type fly pattern into the shallows often works at that time of year.

The lake is only 9 m (29 ft) deep and so the lake is subject to winterkill. Also, summer doldrums set in as the water warms beginning in early July.

To best fish the brook trout, try a worm and bobber or cast a small lure (Panther Martin or Deadly Dick) with a worm. In the spring, focus your efforts at the prominent drop-offs or at the west side of the small island. In the fall, the shallows at the west and east end of the lake as well as the outflow area near the north end are good locations to focus your effort.

Ice fishing season can be very good.

Facilities

There is a rec site at the lake, which provides camping and a cartop boat launch.

Other Options

Some of the better fishing lakes in the area include Nobel Lake (to the northeast), Long Lake (to the southeast) and Pass Lake (to the west). The rainbow can grow quite large in these lakes. Fly fishing in the spring and fall is the preferred fishing method. Be sure to check the regulations for certain restrictions.

Lake Definition

Elevation:	975.6 m (3,200 ft)
Surface Area:	14 ha (35 ac)
Mean Depth:	4 m (13 ft)
Max Depth:	8.8 m (29 ft)
Perimeter:	2,092.2 m (6,864 ft)
Way Point:	50° 50' 00" Lat - N 120° 24' 00" Lon - W

Isobel Lake Rec Site

Recent Fish Stocking

Year	Fish Species	Life Stage	Number
1999	eastern brook trout	FG	2,000
1998	eastern brook trout	FG	2,000
1997	eastern brook trout	FG	2,000
1996	eastern brook trout	FG	2,000
1995	eastern brook trout	FG	2,000

To McQueen Lake FSR

Scale

100m   0   100m   200m   300m

Thompson Nicola Region

Little Fort • Isobel Lake • Sicamous / Salmon Arm
Clinton • Cache Creek • Kamloops
Gold Bridge • Lillooet • Merritt
Boston Bar
Spuzzum

Isobel Lake
McQUEEN LAKE FSR
To Hwy 5
McQueen Lake
Griffin Lake
To Kamloops
LAC   DU   BOIS   Rd
Lac du Bois Lake
Pass Lake

Map Courtesy of Backroad Mapbook Volume III Kamloops/Okanagan

Johnson Lake

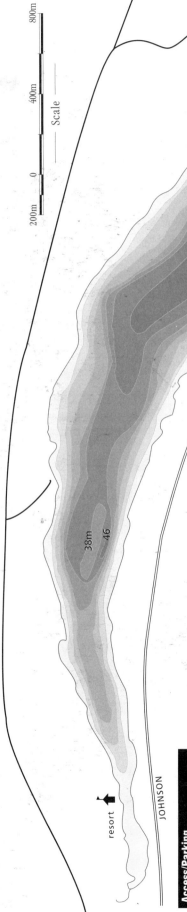

Scale

200m   0   400m   800m

Johnson Lake
Rec Site

30m
22
16
8
38
46m
54
46
38m
46

To
Adams
Lake

FSR

LAKE

JOHNSON

resort

N

Access/Parking

Johnson Lake is easily accessed by taking the Squilax-Anglemont Road leading north from the Trans Canada Highway about 5.5 km northeast of Chase. This paved road immediately crosses a bridge over the Shuswap Lake and then heads north. Soon you will have to turn left at the first major intersection and follow the paved Holdings Road that winds gently along the western banks of the Adams River to the south end of the Adams Lake. Continue northward along the Holdings Road to the mill and from there, an excellent, well graded but windy mainhaul logging road will bring you to the Samatosum Road at the 28.5 km mark. This road switch backs up from the mountainside from Adams Lake. You will soon reach the south end of the lake.

An alternative route is to take the Agate Bay Road, which begins just north of Louis Creek on Highway #5. The Agate Bay Road is paved most of its way. Look for the Johnson Lake Resort sign at the Minova Road junction. Minova Road soon turns into the Johnson Lake Forest Service Road and you are on your way to the west end of the lake. The trip is about 55km from Highway #5.

Fishing

Johnson Lake is known for its super clear, green coloured water found set in a scenic mountainous area. The lake has a sandy bottom and a shallow shoreline. It is not the best of the fishing lakes in this book but the deep water keeps fish active throughout the summer.

Johnson Lake is best fished for rainbow (to 2 kg/5 lbs) by trolling along one of the many drop-offs common to the lake. Trolling a fly on a long leader is productive as are the usual gang trolls.

Fly fishing can still be effective at the outflow near the west end of the lake or near one of the numerous shoals and drop-offs. Try a shrimp, dragonfly or caddisfly pattern for best success. Good fly patterns to try are the fullbacks, half-backs and 52 Buicks.

Shore casting is difficult.

Facilities

Despite the wilderness setting, the **Johnson Lake Rec Site** is not in the prettiest location. There are 6 tables and a cartop boat launch, all found at the eastern end of the lake.

The Johnson Lake Resort (250-828-6966 or www.visualnorth.com/johnsonlake) has 8 rustic cabins for rent as well as ten camping sites located at the west end of the lake. The resort has a convenience store, boat launch, boat rentals, and central washroom with showers and washrooms.

Lake Definition

Elevation:	1,067 m (3,600 ft)
Surface Area:	362 ha (895 ac)
Mean Depth:	17 m (57 ft)
Max Depth:	59 m (193 ft)
Perimeter:	51° 10' 00" Lat - N
Way Point:	119° 46' 00" Lon - W

Recent Fish Stocking

Year	Fish Species	Life Stage	Number
1995	rainbow trout	FF	10,000
1994	rainbow trout	FF	10,000
1993	rainbow trout	FF	5,000

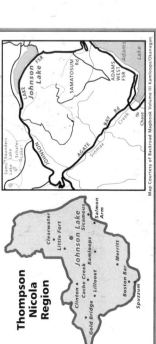

Thompson Nicola Region

Clearwater
Little Fort
Salmon Arm
Johnson Lake
Sicamous
Clinton
Cache Creek
Kamloops
Gold Bridge
Lillooet
Merritt
Boston Bar
Spuzzum

Sam Saunders Lake
Schafer Lake
Johnson Lake
SAMATOSUM Rd
ADAMS WEST FSR
LAKE
FSR
JOHNSON
BAY Rd
AGATE
Simax Creek
To Chase
Adams Lake

Map Courtesy of Backroad Mapbook Volume III Kamloops/Okanagan

Kamloops Lake

Access/Parking

Kamloops is a 25km long lake into which the North and South Thompson Rivers flow. The lake extends from Savona to Kamloops in the east.

The Trans Canada Highway runs along the south shore of the lake providing access along most of the shoreline. The northern shores of the lake are less accessible. The main access is the Sabastion Creek Road leading north from Savona or the Tranquille Road from Kamloops.

Fishing

Kamloops Lake is seldom iced over so it is possible to fish year-round. Despite the close proximity to Kamloops, the lake receives little fishing pressure. That is because the fishing is tough unless you know where to go.

With some luck, it is possible to catch rainbow (1 kg/2 lbs), small kokanee or dollies (to 2 kg/5 lbs) mainly in the early spring to late fall. Trolling is the mainstay of the fishery although fly fishing and spincasting at the river estuaries and at the outflow can be effective.

If you are fishing the kokanee, try a Willow Leaf and worm trolled near the surface (3-9 m/10-30 ft deep) on a very slow troll. Trolling in an "S" manner slows the lure even further while enticing the fish to bite because of the speed fluctuation of the lure.

Rainbow take gang trolls as wells as a variety of plugs and lures such as the Kamlooper, Rapala, Flatfish or Apex. Dollies can be fished effectively at the river estuaries using a bait ball. Trolling with a Flatfish or a Krokodile at the 10-25 m (30-90 ft) level is also effective.

If you want to try a fly, troll a leech, muddler minnow or bucktail.

Facilities

Full facilities are provided along Highway #1. There are also three provincial parks that preserve portions of the shoreline. The Steelhead Provincial Park is located at the southwestern end of the lake at Savona. That park has camping and picnicing facilities as well as a wharf and boat launch. Painted Bluffs Provincial Park is found on the northern shores of the lake near Cooper Creek. This new provincial park preserves a series of Indian Pictographs but does not have any facilities. The third park is the Lac Du Bois Grassland Provincial Park found at the northeastern end of the lake to the west of Kamloops. Although there are camping facilities in the park towards the north end, there are no facilities situated on Kamloops Lake.

The Lakeside Country Inn (1-800-909-7434) offers luxury accommodation at a beautiful lakeside resort.

Lake Definition

Elevation: 343 m (1,125 ft)
Surface Area: 5,584.8 ha (13,800 ac)
Mean Depth: 74.1 m (243 ft)
Max Depth: 150.9 m (495 ft)
Way Point: 50° 44' 00" Lat - N
120° 38' 00" Lon - W

Thompson Nicola Region

Little Fort
Sicamous
Salmon Arm
Cache Creek
Kamloops
Clinton
Merritt
Lillooet
Gold Bridge
Kamloops Lake
Boston Bar
Spuzzum

North Thompson River
Tranquille
River
Kamloops
Frederick
Kamloops Lake
Copper Creek
Savona
To Cache Creek

Grasslands Provincial Park

S. Thompson R.

Tranquille
Tranquille River
ROAD

To Abbey Rd

Frederick
FREDERICK

Battle Bluff

Cherry Bluff
Cherry Creek
Cherry Cr
Duffy Cr
To Kamloops

Red Point

Rosseau Cr

Painted Bluffs Provincial Park
Painted Bluffs
Copper Creek
Carabine Cr

Six Mile Point

Brussels Cr

Sabiston Cr

Durand Cr

Savona
Steelhead Provincial Park
To Cache Creek
Thompson River

N

Scale
1km 0 1km 2km 3km 4km 5km

Kane Lakes

Access/Parking

These pothole lakes are set in the beautiful Kane Valley. Trembling aspen, vast meadows and range land and rolling hills highlight the valley.

You can access the Kane Valley lakes by RV or car if you want. From Merritt, head southeast on the Okanagan Connector. Just north of Corbett Lake, the Kane Valley Road heads southwest. The road is well signed so simply follow the direction to the Kane Valley X-C Ski Trials and you will reach the lakes.

From the Coquihalla Highway, take the Coldwater Road Exit (Exit 256) and head north on a paved secondary road to Kingsvale. You will cross a bridge in Kingsvale and head up a hill where the road turns to gravel. Take the first major right and you will be driving under the Coquihalla Highway on the Kane Valley Road. Stay on the main road all the way to the lakes.

Fishing

Kane Lakes are comprised of two small lakes ideal for fly fishing given their nice shoals. The lakes are only 10 m (30-35 ft) deep so they are not well suited for trolling. Flyfish and spincasting is you're best bet but be warned, the fishing is quite spotty for the rainbow and brook trout that reach 2 kg (4 lbs).

When fly fishing the dark, nutrient rich waters, try matching the caddisfly or mayfly hatch. In the fall, elk wing caddis flies, Tom thumb, leech and Doc Spratley patterns are preferred. At other times of the year, attractor type patterns like a leech, Doc Spratley or Wooley Bugger is worth trying. Focus your efforts around the islands in the southern most lake.

The lake is stocked annually and there is a bait and ice-fishing ban at the lake. Also, there is a two trout limit and a single barbless hook requirement.

Spring and fall is the best times to fish because the shallow waters warm in the summer and the fish become inactive.

Facilities

Kane Lake Rec Site has 5 camping units scattered on the south end of the Kane Lakes. These sites receive heavy use during the summer primarily by fishermen. The rec site is very scenic set next to the bullrushes on the lake. A deteriorating wharf is available as is a cartop boat launch and picnic tables.

Other Options

The next page describes some of the excellent **Kane Valley Chain** fishing lakes found immediately to the west.

Further southwest, the Vough Valley Road gives access to another series of good fishing lakes. **Shea, Boss, Tahla** and **Davis Lakes** all offer beautiful campsites and good rainbow trout fishing. Trolling is the most popular method but fly fishing in the spring and fall can be productive.

Thompson Nicola Region

Map Courtesy of Backroad Mapbook Volume III Kamloops/Okanagan

Lake Definition (No. 1 Lake)

Elevation: 1,067 m (3,500.6 ft)
Surface Area: 7.7 ha (19 ac)
Mean Depth: 5.2 m (17 ft)
Max Depth: 9.5 m (31.2 ft)
Perimeter: 1,325.8 m (4,349.7 ft)
Way Point: 49° 59' 00" Lat - N
120° 41' 00" Lon - W

Lake Definition (No. 2 Lake)

Elevation: 1,067 m (3,501 ft)
Surface Area: 9 ha (22.2 ac)
Mean Depth: 5.5 m (18 ft)
Max Depth: 10.7 m (35.1 ft)
Perimeter: 1,645.9 m (5,399.9 ft)

Recent Fish Stocking (No.1 Lake)

Year	Fish Species	Life Stage	Number
1997	rainbow trout	YE	2,000
1996	rainbow trout	YE	1,500
1995	rainbow trout	YE	2,000

Recent Fish Stocking (No.2 Lake)

Year	Fish Species	Life Stage	Number
1997	rainbow trout	YE	1,500
1996	rainbow trout	FF	1,500
1995	rainbow trout	YE	2,000

Kane Lake No. 2

Kane Lake No. 1

Kane Lakes X-C Ski Trails

Kane Lakes Rec Site

N

Scale

Kane Valley Chain Lakes

Access/Parking

These pothole lakes are set in the beautiful Kane Valley. Trembling aspen, vast meadows and range land and rolling hills highlight the valley.

You can access the Kane Valley lakes by RV or car if you want. From Merritt, head southeast on the Okanagan Connector. Just north of Corbett Lake, the Kane Valley Road heads southwest. The road is well signed so simply follow the direction to the Kane Valley X-C Ski Trials and you will reach the lakes.

From the Coquihalla Highway, take the Coldwater Road Exit (Exit 256) and head north on a paved secondary road to Kingsvale. You will cross a bridge in Kingsvale and head up a hill where the road turns to gravel. Take the first major right and you will be driving under the Coquihalla Highway on the Kane Valley Road. Stay on the main road all the way to the lakes.

Lake Definition (Harmon Lake)

Surface Area: 21.4 ha (52.9 ac)
Mean Depth: 8.4 m (27.6 ft)
Max Depth: 19.2 m (63 ft)
Perimeter: 2,834 m (9,300 ft)
Way Point: 49° 58' 10" Lat - N
120° 44' 58" Lon - W

Lake Definition (Englishmen Lk)

Surface Area: 13.4 ha (33.1 ac)
Mean Depth: 3.2 m (10.5 ft)
Max Depth: 8.5 m (27.9 ft)
Perimeter: 1,829 m (6,000 ft)

Lake Definition (No. 1 Lake)

Surface Area: 1.6 ha (4 ac)
Mean Depth: 5.8 m (19 ft)
Max Depth: 10 m (32.8 ft)
Perimeter: 567 m (1,860 ft)

Fishing

Englishmann Lake is being intensively managed so that there is now some reasonably good fly fishing for rainbow trout to 1 kg (2 lbs) in size. The lake is only 8.5 m (28 ft) deep so the water warms in the summer leaving spring and fall the best times to fish. The lake has extensive shoals covered by thick aquatic vegetation ideal for insect growth and fish habitat. For best results, try casting a fly towards the many weed beds that line the lake.

Mayfly, dragonfly nymph and damselfly nymph patterns are very good in the spring. In the fall, try a Doc Spratley, boatman imitation, leech, Tom thumb or a 52 Buick.

Given the depth of the lake, trolling is very limited as anything trolled at 3 m (10 ft) will become weedy in no time. You can troll a fly near the surface, however.

The lake has a two trout limit, bait ban, single barbless hook restriction and an ice fishing ban.

Harmon Lake is the most popular lake found in the Kane Valley and receives heavy fishing pressure throughout the ice-free season. Rainbows to 1.5 kg are taken consistently. The lake is usually fly fished at the southwest end of the main body of the lake. Some fly fishermen try casting in the southwest bay but the water is only 6 m (20 ft) deep making the fish spooky.

Trollers circle the main part of the lake around the drop off. Gang trolls such as the Willow Leaf and worm are the most effective method of trolling but using a small lure such as a Deadly Dick or Flat fish or a fly such as a Muddler Minnow or Leech should not be ruled out.

For fly fishing, a chironomid papae fished near the bottom on a slow retrieval is very productive in June. Dragonfly and damselfly nymphs work well in late June to early July. In the fall, try a 52 Buick, Doc Spratley, leech or a water boatman imitation.

Facilities

Harmon Lake Rec Sites are comprised of 2 different sites totalling 34 camping units. The eastern most site is located in an open range land and is often windswept whereas the western most site is more sheltered and found within the trees. Both sites receive very heavy use because Harmon Lake is extremely popular with fishermen. There is a cartop boat launch at both sites as well as picnic tables.

Recent Fish Stocking (Harmon Lake)

Year	Fish Species	Life Stage	Number
1997	rainbow trout	YE	6,000
1996	rainbow trout	YE	6,000
1995	rainbow trout	YE	4,000

Recent Fish Stocking (Englishman Lake)

Year	Fish Species	Life Stage	Number
1997	rainbow trout	YE	2,000
1996	rainbow trout	YE, FG	3,500
1995	rainbow trout	YE	2,000

Harmon Lake Rec Site

N

3
6
9m
12
15
18m

6m

6 3

Harmon Lake

ROAD

VALLEY

KANE

9m
6
3

No. 1 Lake

6

3m

Englishmen Lake

Thompson Nicola Region

Little Fort
Sicamous
Salmon Arm
Clinton
Cache Creek
Kamloops
Gold Bridge
Lillooet
Merritt
Boston Bar
Spuzzum
Kane Valley Chain Lakes

To Merritt
Corbett Lake
Courtney
Rd
97C
5A
Inmish Lake
To Princeton
Menzies Lake
Kane Lakes
KANE VALLEY
Roth Lake
Harmon Lake
Englishmen Lake

Map Courtesy of Backroad Mapbook Volume III Kamloops/Okanagan

100m   0   100m   200m   300m   400m   500m
Scale

Kentucky Lake

The map area shows:

Kentucky-Alleyne Rec Area

6m, 12, 6, 36m, 30, 24, 18, 24m, 30, 36m, 6, 12, 12, 18, 6m, 9

To Bates Road

N

100m 0 100m 200m 300m 400m 500m

Scale

Lake Definition

Elevation:	991 m (3,251 ft)
Surface Area:	36 ha (89 ac)
Mean Depth:	16.5 m (54 ft)
Max Depth:	41 m (134.5 ft)
Perimeter:	5,259 m (17,250 ft)
Way Point:	49° 54' 00" Lat - N
	120° 34' 00" Lon - W

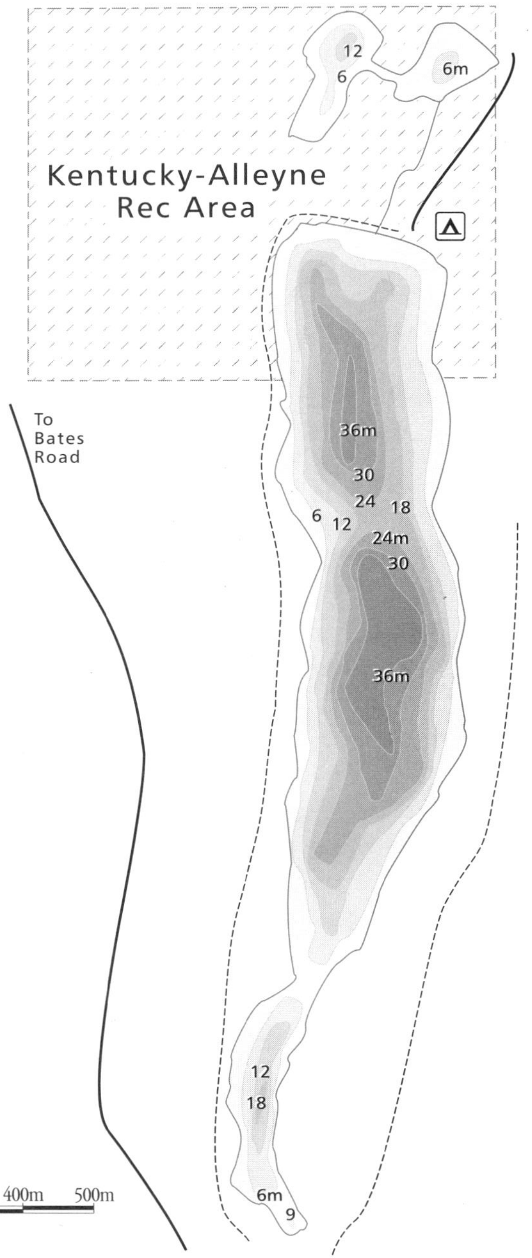

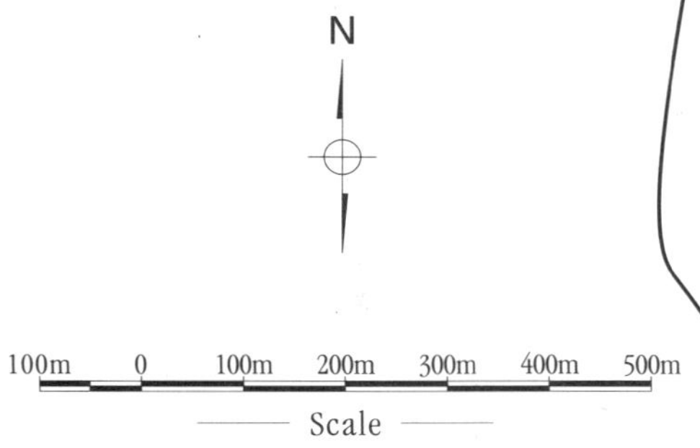

Access/Parking

Kentucky Lake is found within the beautiful Kentucky-Alleyne Recreation Area. The recreation area is highlighted by open rangeland with encroaching forests. Several small lakes dot the landscape. The recreation area is very popular throughout the summer months given the good fishing and the scenic surroundings. There are several different lakes to choose from in the area but Kentucky Lake is one of the most popular.

Kentucky Lake is easily accessed off the Bates Road, a good 2wd road. Bates Road can either be found by heading southwest from the Loon Lake interchange on the Okanagan Connector or by heading south on Highway 5A from the Aspen Grove Interchange and taking a left once you reach the Bates Road turn-off. Once on Bates Road, you will soon reach the north end of Kentucky Lake so long as you remain on the main road.

Access is good enough to bring a car or truck with a small trailer.

Fishing

Kentucky Lake receives heavy fishing pressure all the way from ice-off in mid-April to ice-on in November. As a result, the fishing tends to be slow so you are going to have to work hard for one of the rainbow.

The fish grow rapidly so a 2 kg (3-5 lbs) rainbow is not uncommon. This is because of the abundance of freshwater shrimp and aquatic insects such as the chironomids (midges).

The lake is deep enough (40 m /133 ft) that trolling is effective. Most fishermen drag a gang troll (Ford Fender or Willow Leaf with worm) or small lure/spinner (Panther Martin, Flatfish or Deadly Dick) behind their boat.

The lake has some nice shoals particularly near the south end of the lake between the main body of the lake and the bay. Also, drop-offs line most of the main body of the clear lake. Fly fishermen and spincasters should try near these areas.

The usual hatches of the region are found here so try to match the hatch. The chironomid hatch in June is definitely worth trying. In the fall try leetches, Doc Spratleys, wooly buggers or dragon nymphs.

Facilities

Kentucky Lake is located in the heart of the 144 ha Kentucky-Alleyne Provincial Park. The popularity of the provincial park is steadily increasing, but you are still likely to find a spot in the 63 vehicle/tent campsite throughout the summer months except the long weekend. At the park, you will find a 4 km trail that circles Kentucky Lake providing access for shore fishing or a pleasant family walk. There are not as many facilities at this park as compared to other parks in the Okanagan (no showers, sani-station or flush toilets) so you should expect a more rustic setting.

Other Options

Several lakes are found in the area. **Alleyne** and **Bluey Lakes** are highlighted earlier in this book. You can also try **Crater Lake**. This lake offers surprisingly good fishing for smaller rainbow that can reach 2 kg (5 lbs) in size. Trolling is the mainstay of the lake but fly fishermen should not be discouraged. The lake is 20 ha in size.

Kidd Lake is found next to Highway #5A but still produces well for stocked rainbow to 1 kg (2 lbs). The lake is best fished from a float tube.

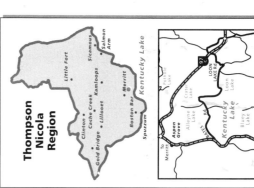

Thompson Nicola Region

Little Fort, Sicamous, Salmon Arm, Clinton, Cache Creek, Kamloops, Lillooet, Merritt, Gold Bridge, Boston Bar, Spuzzum, Kentucky Lake

To Merritt, Aspen Grove, Crater Lake, Alleyne Lake, Loon Lake, Kentucky Lake, Bluey Lake, To Princeton

Courtesy of Backroad Mapbook Volume III Kamloops/Okanagan

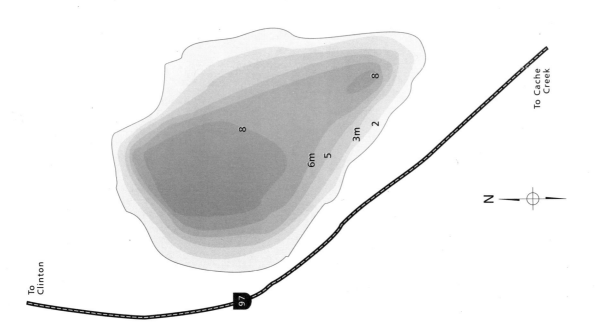

To Clinton

To Cache Creek

N

Scale

100m 0 100m 200m 300m 400m

Kersey (5 Mile) Lake

...e lake located in the heart of cattle ...ake, drive north of Cache Creek on ...ariboo Highway (Highway #97). The lake is right next to the highway south of Clinton. The exit to the lake is well signed as a provincial park surrounds the lake.

Facilities

The provincial park provides day-use facilities and a boat launch.

Other Options

Three Mile Lake is found further north along Highway 97. This small, deep 15 ha lake has brook trout to 0.5 kg (1 lb) that are best caught with a float and bait or by ice fishing in winter. The lake does not receive a lot of fishing pressure even though it is found next to the highway and can be fished from shore.

Lake Definition

Surface Area: 23 ha (56.8 ac)
Mean Depth: 4.8 m (15.7 ft)
Max Depth: 9.1 m (29.9 ft)
Perimeter: 2,134 m (7,000 ft)
Way Point: 51° 02' 00" Lat - N
121° 33' 00" Lon - W

Fishing

Kersey Lake is unique because it has a good fishery for eastern brook trout. The lake is only 10 m (30 ft) deep near its center so the lake warms in the summer months severely affecting fishing success.

At 925 m (3035 ft) in elevation, ice-off is in late April. After the lake turns over, the brook trout begin to bite on small lures and worms (Deadly Dick or Wedding Ring) cast near the drop-offs that circle the lake. It is possible to troll the lures in a circular manner around the lake so long as you stay shallow.

Fly fishing is not very productive in the spring. In the fall, however, the eastern brook trout congregate in the shallows for spawning. At that time, the aggressive males bite any attractor type fly pattern such as a Wooley Bugger, Doc Spratley or Muddler Minnow. Spincasting in the shallows in the fall is also a good bet.

In the winter months, ice fishing with hook and bait is highly productive.

Recent Fish Stocking

Year	Fish Species	Life Stage	Number
1997	brook trout	FG	1,000
1996	EB	FG	1,000
1995	EB	FG	1,000

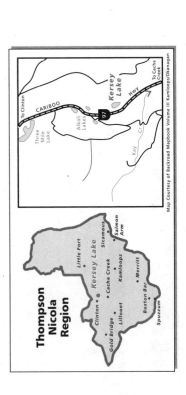

Thompson Nicola Region

Little Fort
Clinton • Kersey Lake • Sicamous
Cache Creek • Salmon Arm
Gold Bridge • Kamloops
Lillooet • Merritt
Boston Bar
Spuzzum

To Clinton
CARIBOO
Three Mile Lake
Alkali Lake
Kersey Lake
Hwy 97
To Cache Creek
Kay Cr.

Map Courtesy of Backroad Mapbook Volume III Kamloops/Okanagan

Knouff (Sullivan) Lake

Access/Parking

This lake is locally known as Knouff Lake but is officially renamed Sullivan Lake after the family that owned property on the lake for many year. To find the lake, head north on Highway #5 from Kamloops. Take the Sun Peaks Road exit heading east and then either the first major road to the north (Sullivan Valley Road) or the second one (Knouff Lake Road). Both are good logging roads leading to the south end of Knouff Lake. RV's and large trailers can access the lake from this access route.

An alternative, steeper route is to drive north on Highway #5 past the Sun Peaks Road and take a right on the Vinsulla-Knouff Lake Road. Stay on the main road for 12 km and you will reach Knouff Lake.

Fishing

Knouff Lake offers good fishing for rainbow trout from May to October by fly fishing or trolling. The rainbow range in the 1-3 kg (2-6 lb) range with 4-7 kg (8 to 16 lb) fish not uncommon. The North American record of 7.8 kg (17.25 lbs) for a dry fly was caught at Knouff lake.

For fly fishermen, try casting a fly near one of the many shoals or sunken islands that are easily seen through the clear water. Also, match one of the sedge, mayfly damselfly or chironomid hatches. The flies of choice at the lake are the Knouff Lake Special, leech patterns, damselfly patterns, shrimp patterns, mayfly nymph, dragonfly patterns, sedge patterns and the Doc Spratley. In particular, the late evening sedge hatch can be a dynamite time to fish.

Trollers use a Willow Leaf or Ford Fender with a worm. Trolling a froggy, silver & black or gold Flatfish is also effective.

Facilities

The Sullivan Lake Recreation Site is found across the road from the lake, which is commonly referred to as Knouff Lake. The rec site offers 4 picnic tables and a seperate cartop boat launch.

The Knouff Lake Resort (1-888-562-0555) has 11 rustic, one-bedroom cabins with electricity, fridge and wood burning stove but without linen, running water, kitchen utensils. A communal washroom, showers and laundry facilities are offered as well as serviced camping sites for RVs and more quaint tenting pads. A convenience store and boat rentals are also at the resort, which is open year round.

Other Options

Little Knouff, **Badger**, **Little Badger** and **Spooney Lakes** are all found north of Knouff Lake. These lakes all offer good rainbow fishing, especially in the spring and fall. The Knouff Lake Road provides access to the area. You can find more information on Badger Lake and area on page 8.

Another option is **Community Lake**. This 36 ha lake is found along a side road 9 km north of the Sun Peaks Road on the Knouff Lake Road. Turn right and continue 6 km to the rec site.

Lake Definition

Elevation:	1,149 m (3,768 ft)
Surface Area:	102.63 ha (253.6 ac)
Mean Depth:	9.5 m (31.2 ft)
Max Depth:	24.1 m (79 ft)
Perimeter:	50° 58' 00" Lat - N
Way Point:	120° 07' 00" Lon - W

Recent Fish Stocking

Year	Fish Species	Life Stage	Number
1999	Rainbow Trout	YE	5,000
1998	Rainbow Trout	YE	5,000
1997	Rainbow Trout	YE	7,000

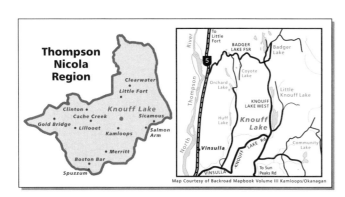

Thompson Nicola Region

Map Courtesy of Backroad Mapbook Volume III Kamloops/Okanagan

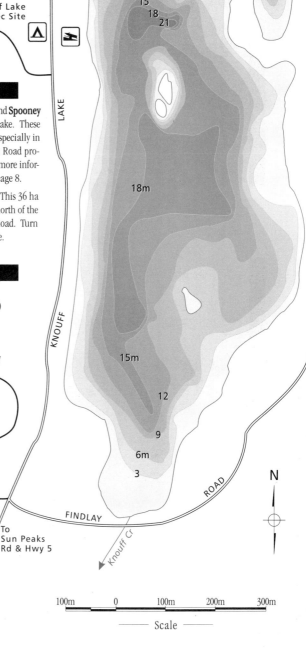

Lac Le Jeune Lake

...lly called Fish Lake but was ...e Jeune in the late 1800's. The ...ery popular year round destination for all types of outdoor recreationists. The lake is surrounded by a lodge-pole pine, Douglas-fir and spruce forest on the north and south sides whereas the west end of the lake has a shallow bay with a heavy growth of aquatic vegetation.

The lake is 20 minutes south of Kamloops and is easily accessed by taking the Lac Le Jeune Exit (Exit 336) on the Coquihalla Connector between Merritt and Kamloops. Head east on the paved, Lac Le Jeune Road and within 4km, you will see the turn-off to the lake.

Facilities

Lac Le Jeune Provincial Park has a total of 144 camp spots, which are open from April to October. There is also a very large picnic area and paved boat launch in the park. The provincial park is extremely popular for camping, boating, swimming and fishing. Hikers, mountain bikers and cross-country skiers all take advantage of the excellent trail system surrounding the lake.

There are several resorts as well as some private cabins on the lake. The Wildflower Guesthouse offers accommodations in a small log cabin as well as fishing packages with guiding services. Lac Le Jeune Resort (1-800-561-5253 or vjpresorts@kamloops.com), at the southwest end, is one of the nicer resorts in the area. Fishing packages are available including guiding services. Woody Life Village Resort (250-374-3833) was built in 1990 on Woody Pond bird sanctuary. The resort has modern log cabins along with a restaurant, indoor pool, spa and exercise room.

Fishing

Lac Le Jeune offers reasonably good fishing beginning at ice-off in late April to early May. The rainbow grow to 2 kg (5 lbs) but tend to be pan size.

The deep, clear waters are nutrient rich allowing fast growth of the fish. Good thing, because without the intense stocking program in place and the rapid fish growth, the fishing would drop off quickly because of overfishing.

By far the most popular method of fishing is trolling with trolls and small lures (Flatfish, Apex or Deadly Dick). Fly fishermen should not be discouraged as the lake has a many bays, weed beds, drop-offs and shoals ideal for casting a fly. Try fishing the lake during the sedge hatch beginning in late June or during the mayfly hatch in late June to early July. There is also a decent chironomid hatch in May- early June. Damselfly and dragonfly nymph patterns work well throughout the spring and fall when thrown towards the reeds on the west and east side of the lake.

Since the lake is relatively deep (maximum 27 m/88 ft), the water remains cool enough to allow fishing to be active throughout the summer months.

Lake Definition

Elevation:	1,183.5 m (3,883 ft)
Surface Area:	149.3 ha (368.9 ac)
Mean Depth:	6.7 m (22.1 ft)
Max Depth:	17.7 m (58 ft)
Perimeter:	10,076.8 m (33,960 ft)
Way Point:	51° 14' 00" Lat - N
	120° 21' 00" Lon - W

Recent Fish Stocking

Year	Fish Species	Life Stage	Number
1999	rainbow trout	YE	15,000
1997	rainbow trout	YE	15,000
1996	rainbow trout	YE	15,000
1995	rainbow trout	YE	15,000

Thompson Nicola Region

Little Fort
Sicamous
Salmon Arm
Clinton
Cache Creek
Kamloops
Gold Bridge
Lillooet
Lac Le Jeune
Merritt
Boston Bar
Spuzzum

To Kamloops
Stake Lake
LAC LE JEUNE RD
Lac Le Jeune
Shambrook Lake
Walloper Lake
To Merritt
Map Courtesy of Backroad Mapbook Volume III Kamloops/Okanagan

To Lac Le Jeune Road

Lac Le Jeune Provincial Park

3m
6
9m
12
15
18m
27m
24
18 21m
15
12
9 6m
3
6m
3

resort

Meadow Cr

N

Scale
100m 0 100m 200m 300m 400m 500m

Laurel Lake

Access/Parking

Laurel Lake is one of a series of small lakes east of Little Fort off Highway #24.

Follow Highway #24 until you reach the Taweel Road. Head north and Laurel Lake is off to the right and can be reached by a short hike.

The southern tip of the lake is also within a short walk of the highway.

Fishing

Laurel Lake, like other lakes in the area, is a productive fly fishing lake with many small rainbow. The fish can reach 2 kg (5 lbs) but that is a rarity.

The lake is 17 m (55 ft) deep towards the middle but averages only 5.5 m (18 ft) deep. Extensive shallows are found at the south end of the lake. Try spincasting or fly fishing near the drop-offs and the deep pothole. Any one of a number of small lures or spinners works.

For fly fishermen, the common trout fly patterns all work. A nymph pattern sunk near the drop-offs is always a good choice.

The lake, given its depth, tends to suffer from the summer slowdown.

Facilities

There are no facilities at the lake but several campgrounds are found nearby.

Other Options

North of Highway 24 there are several small lakes for you to explore. In particular, **Walkin**, **Nora** and **Deer Lakes** are good rainbow lakes. The trout, which can reach 1 kg (2 lbs), can be taken by spin casting or fly fishing.

Lake Definition

Elevation: 1,372 m (4,500 ft)
Surface Area: 57 ha (140 ac)
Mean Depth: 5.5 m (18 ft)
Max Depth: 17 m (55 ft)
Perimeter: 4,184.3 m (13,728 ft)
Way Point: 51° 31' 00" Lat - N
120° 22' 00" Lon - W

15m
12
9m
6
3m

N

Scale

500m   0   1 km   2km

TAWEEL

Rd

To
Hwy 24

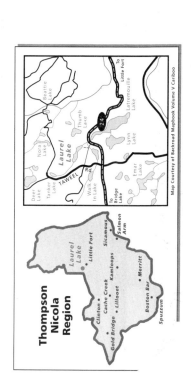

Map Courtesy of Backroad Mapbook Volume V Cariboo

Thompson Nicola Region

Little Shuswap Lake

… fronts the town of Chase and is … Highway as you are driving east … Sorrento and Salmon Arm. The southwest end of the lake is easily accessed by driving into Chase and heading for the water. The northeast end is reached by taking the Squilax-Anglemont Road over the Shuswap River and then heading west on the Little Shuswap Road.

Fishing

Little Shuswap Lake is 1800 ha in size and is at the 345 m (1130 ft) elevation level. Like the Shuswap Lake, this lake offers reasonable fishing for rainbows to 5 kg (10 lbs) primarily by trolling.

In the late spring (May and June), fishing is at its best given the fact that the rainbow are actively feeding near the surface on salmon fry before the salmon fry return to the ocean. To take advantage of the feed, it is best to troll a silver bucktail or silver spoon quickly on the surface. Often times, the salmon fry hold up in small bays and fly fishing or spincasting in these areas is very effective.

By the summertime, the rainbows and lake trout creep to the depths as the water warms. It is best to troll with a downrigger at 10-25 m (30-90 ft) using a plug, Apex or Flatfish.

In October-November, the fishing picks up again with trolling bucktails, Apex or a plug near the surface being the most effective method of catching the rainbow and lake char. If you are lucky, you may be able to hook one of the big Chinook salmon that pass through the lake on the way to the spawning grounds.

There is a small population of kokanee as well as some dolly vardens. For kokanee, the best fishing begins in July and extends into August. The fish are easily caught using a wedding ring with a maggot or a worm trolled dead slow near the surface. If you catch one kokanee, chances are, you have found a school of kokanee so it is best to troll over the same area continuously for best results.

Spincasters and fly fishermen should focus their effort at the outflow to the South Thompson River.

Please note that the northeastern end of the lake is closed to fishing.

Facilities

The Little Shuswap Park, at the southwest end of the lake in Chase, offers a boat launch, beach and picnic site. There is private camping along the lake as well as numerous private residences. The lake is very popular in the summer primarily because of watersports. If you plan to stay at the lake you should reserve a space before heading out.

Lake Definition

Elevation: 346.6 m (1,137 ft)
Surface Area: 1,814 ha (4,480 ft)
Mean Depth: 14 m (47 ft)
Max Depth: 59 m (195 ft)
Way Point: 50° 51' 00" Lat - N
119° 38' 00" Lon - W

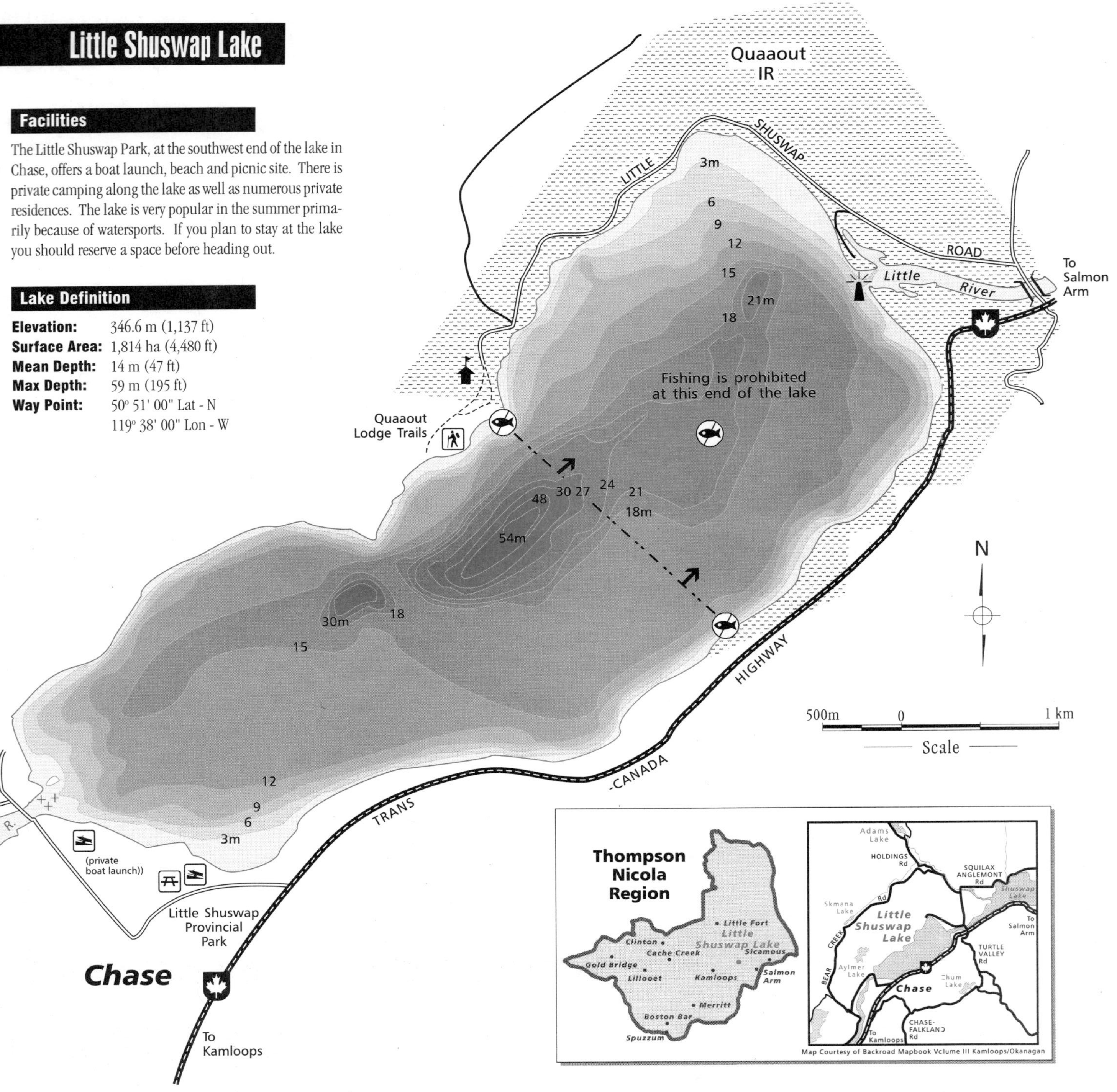

Quaaout IR
Little Shuswap Road
Little River
To Salmon Arm
Fishing is prohibited at this end of the lake
Quaaout Lodge Trails
Trans-Canada Highway
Shuswap Rd
South Thompson R.
(private boat launch))
Little Shuswap Provincial Park
Chase
To Kamloops
3m
6
9
12
15
18
21m
24
21
18m
30 27
48
54m
30m
15
N
500m
0
1 km
Scale
Thompson Nicola Region
Little Fort
Little Shuswap Lake
Clinton
Cache Creek
Sicamous
Gold Bridge
Lillooet
Kamloops
Salmon Arm
Merritt
Boston Bar
Spuzzum
Adams Lake
Holdings Rd
Squilax Anglemont Rd
Shuswap Lake
Skmana Lake
Little Shuswap Lake
To Salmon Arm
Turtle Valley Rd
Bear Creek
Aylmer Lake
Chum Lake
Chase
Chase-Falkland Rd
To Kamloops
Map Courtesy of Backroad Mapbook Volume III Kamloops/Okanagan

Lodgepole Lake

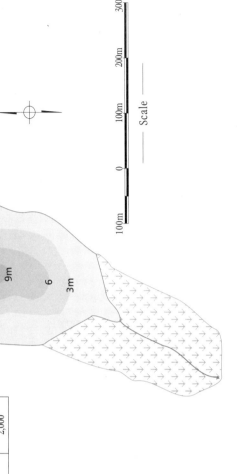

Access/Parking

Lodgepole Lake is one of the many good fishing lakes found in the Lac Le Jeune area.

Lodgepole Lake is found on the east side of the Coquihalla Connector east of the State-McConnell Rec Area. Take the Lac Le Jeune Exit (Exit 336) and head north to State Lake. You will find the Chewhels Mnt Road leading west from the north end of State Lake. Follow that road under the Coquihalla Connector and soon you will reach the north end of Lodgepole Lake.

Fishing

Lodgepole Lake is at 1433 m (4700 ft) in elevation and the fishing for the rainbow does not begin until mid to late May but the summer fishery usually remains active. The rainbow average 0.75 kg (1-2 lbs) but the odd one reaches 2.5 kg (5-7 lbs).

Fly fishing is the mainstay of the lake with dragonfly nymph and shrimp patterns being the most consistent flies. Fish the shrimp patterns near the bottom on a fast sinking line whereas with the dragonfly nymph patterns, cast them towards the drop-offs at the west and east ends of the lake. The shoal areas at the north and south end also look inviting.

Spincasting a small lure such as a Flatfish or Deadly Dick is productive when cast near the drop-offs.

The lake is only 11 m (35 ft) deep so there has been a real problem with winterkill. However, an aerator has been installed and so the problem has been reduced.

Please note that there is an electric motor only restriction on the lake.

Facilities

Lodgepole Lake Rec Site is a small (10 unit) rec site used primarily by fishermen or visitors to the Chewhels Mountain Motorcycle Trails. A cartop boat launch allows fishing at the lake.

Other Options

Lodgepole Lake is found close to the popular fishing areas of **McConnell**, **Stake**, **Lac Le Jeune** and **Walloper Lakes**. All of these lakes are highlighted in this book.

Lake Definition

Elevation: m
Surface Area: ha
Mean Depth: m
Max Depth: m
Perimeter: m
Way Point: 50° 31' 00" Lat - N
120° 31' 00" Lon - W

Recent Fish Stocking

Year	Fish Species	Life Stage	Number
1999	rainbow trout	YE	2,000
1998	rainbow trout	YE	2,000
1997	rainbow trout	YE	2,000
1996	rainbow trout	YE	4,000
1995	rainbow trout	YE	2,000

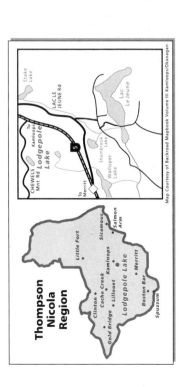

Logan Lake

To Kamloops

ROAD

CREEK

MEADOW

To Logan Lake

N

2
3m
5
6m
8
6m
5
3m
2

Scale

100m 0 100m 200m 300m 400m 500m

To Kamloops
MEADOW Cr Rd
Logan Lake
Logan Lake
97C
TUNKWA LAKE Rd
To Ashcroft
To Merritt

Thompson Nicola Region

Little Fort
Salmon Arm
Sicamous
Cache Creek Kamloops
Clinton
Gold Bridge
Lillooet
Logan Lake
Merritt
Boston Bar
Spuzzum

Access/Parking

The town of Logan Lake was built because of a nearby mine. The lake is a short, 1 km drive from downtown Logan Lake east on the Meadow Creek Road.

To reach Logan Lake, either head north on Highway 97C from Merritt or southeast from Ashcroft. You can also reach the lake by travelling south on the Tunkwa Lake Road from Savona. Yet another option is to take the Lac Le Jeune Exit (Exit 336) off the Coquihalla Connector south of Kamloops and head west on the Meadow Creek Road to the lake.

A car or RV can reach the lake.

Fishing

The ice melts off the lake in mid-April to early May, reforming in mid to late December. An aerator has been installed at the lake to prevent winterkill because the lake is only 8 m (26 ft) deep.

The lake offers good fishing for rainbow trout to 2+ kg (average 20-25 cm/8-10"). The numbers are maintained with an annual stocking program as well as a spawning channel that sees spawning activity in May-June. The nutrient rich waters of the lake ensure that the fish grow rapidly.

While sampling the lake, you will see both trollers and fly fishermen. The lake contains leeches, dragonflies and freshwater shrimp. Also, there are good hatches of caddisflies, damselflies, chironomids and mayflies throughout the year. Try matching one of those hatches or use an attractor type fly pattern like a Doc Spratley or a Carey Special.

To maintain the fish stock, the lake has a single barbless hook restriction, electric motor only restriction and there is a limit of two trout per day.

Facilities

At the lake, you will find a day use area together with a 24 site Municipal campsite complete with flush toilets, water taps, firewood, hot showers and some power. A nature trail around the lake provides access for shore fishing.

Logan Lake Lodge (250-523-9466 or pgm@istar.ca) is found in the town center across from the lake. Unlike the more remote resorts in the Thompson/Nicola area, this resort is a hotel with such amenities as TV, telephones, full bath, pub and family restaurant. The rooms are offered at a reasonable rate.

Lake Definition

Elevation:	1,037 m (3,400 ft)
Surface Area:	11.5 ha (28.4 ac)
Mean Depth:	3.5 m (11.4 ft)
Max Depth:	8 m (26 ft)
Perimeter:	2,075.7 m (6,810 ft)
Way Point:	50° 30' 00" Lat - N
	120° 48' 00" Lon - W

Recent Fish Stocking

Year	Fish Species	Life Stage	Number
1999	rainbow trout	YE, FG	1500
1998	rainbow trout	YE, FG, CA*	5,483
1997	rainbow trout	YE, FG	4,004
1996	rainbow trout	YE, FG	2319
1995	rainbow trout	YE, FG	3,000

*CA=CATCHABLES

Lost Horse Lake

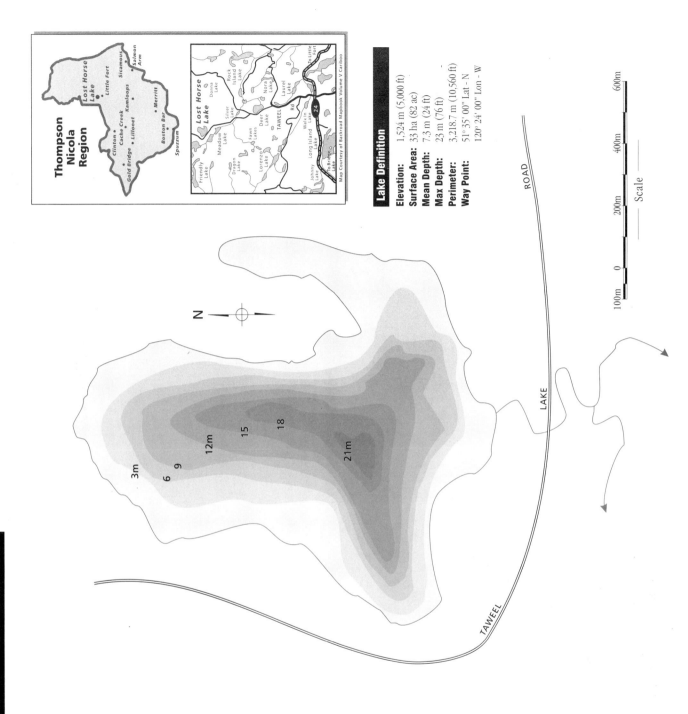

Thompson Nicola Region

Map Courtesy of Backroad Mapbook Volume V Cariboo

Lake Definition

Elevation: 1,524 m (5,000 ft)
Surface Area: 33 ha (82 ac)
Mean Depth: 7.3 m (24 ft)
Max Depth: 23 m (76 ft)
Perimeter: 3,218.7 m (10,560 ft)
Way Point: 51° 35' 00" Lat - N
120° 24' 00" Lon - W

— Scale —

100m 0 200m 400m 600m

Access/Parking

Lost Horse Lake is one of many pothole lakes located west of Little Fort. To reach the lake, turns left on Highway #24 at Little Fort and continue on the highway until you reach the Taweel Lake Road. Head north on this road past a series of small lakes. Avoid the Blowdown Road turn-off a kilometer from the highway and then stay left all the way to the lake. The rough road will bring you right next to the western shores of the lake. The lake is nearby to Meadow and Flapjack Lakes and north of Deer Lake.

The Taweel Lake Road is a bit rough in places so a 4wd truck is a definite advantage.

Fishing

Lost Horse Lake is worth trying as the lake has good fishing for rainbow that reach 1 kg (2-3 lbs). The lake has a nice bay at the southeast end with expansive shallows for insect rearing. There are also some inviting shoals at the north end of the lake and productive drop-offs on the eastern and western shores.

The fishing season runs from ice-off in early May to November. The lake does not receive the same intense fishing pressure as other lakes in the area so you can expect some element of solitude when you arrive. Also, the fishing holds through the summer as the lake is fairly deep (23 m/76 ft) ensuring the water does not warm significantly during the summer.

Trollers do well with the usual gang trolls or with a Flatfish. Fly fishermen should try the late June-early July caddisfly and mayfly hatches. Try trolling a leech pattern as well.

Spincasters can have good success casting a Deadly Dick, Flatfish, Panther Martin or Blue Fox near the drop-offs. The shoals are also good places to focus.

Facilities

There are no developed facilities at the lake.

Other Options

North of Highway 24 there are several small lakes for you to explore. The deep **Friendly Lake**, the dark watered **Meadow Lake** and **Deer Lake** are good rainbow lakes. The trout, which can reach 2 kg (5 lbs), can be taken by spin casting or fly fishing.

Macheté Lake

Access/Parking

The easiest access is to follow Highway #24 towards the Bridge Lake Store. About 4.5km east of the store, the Machete Lake Road heads south. The lake is about 14 km from Highway #24.

Fishing

Machete Lake provides fair fishing for rainbow trout to 1 kg (2 lbs) in size as well as small kokanee. The fishing begins shortly after ice-off in mid-May and stays steady throughout the season all the way to early November when the lake freezes over. The summer slowdown is not a significant problem as the lake is fairly high in elevation (1100 m/3610 ft) so the water stays cool throughout the year.

The preferred method of fishing is by trolling a lures or leech pattern within 3-5 m (10-15 ft) of the surface. Fly fishermer: should try an attractor type fly pattern such as a Doc Spratley or woolly bugger. Matching the chironomid, damselfly, dragonfly or mayfly hatches can also yield results. Focus your casting around the shoals and drop-offs.

For the kokanee, slowly troll a Willow Leaf and worm, a pink Dick Nite or pink Flatfish.

Please note that the daily limit for kokanee is 2, the lake is closed to fishing from Jan 1-April 30 and there is a single barbless hook restriction.

Facilities

Machete Lake is a popular recreation lake complete with camping, a resort with cabins and boat rentals, picnicking and boat launching facilities.

Other Options

On the way to Macheté Lake, you pass by **Whitley**, **Twin** and **Montana Lakes**. Although these lakes are not known as great fishing lakes, they certainly are worth casting a line into. Similar to most lakes in the area, try fly fishing or spin casting for small rainbow. Winterkill can be a problem in the area.

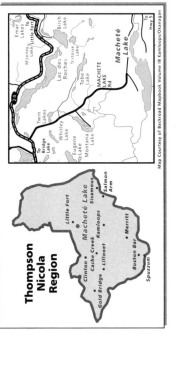

Thompson Nicola Region

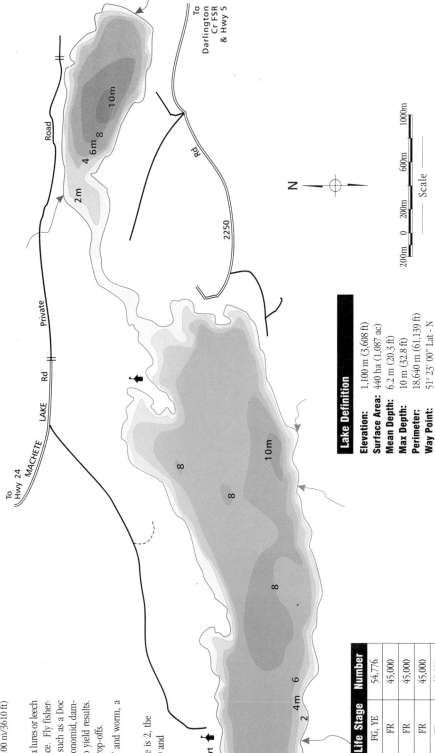

Lake Definition

Elevation:	1,100 m (3,608 ft)
Surface Area:	440 ha (1,087 ac)
Mean Depth:	6.2 m (20.3 ft)
Max Depth:	10 m (32.8 ft)
Perimeter:	18,640 m (61,139 ft)
Way Point:	51° 23' 00" Lat - N
	120° 35' 00" Lon - W

Recent Fish Stocking

Year	Fish Species	Life Stage	Number
1999	rainbow	FG, YE	54,776
1998	kokanee	FR	45,000
1997	kokanee	FR	45,000
1996	kokanee	FR	45,000
1995	kokanee	FR	45,000

Mamit Lake

Access/Parking

Mamit Lake is easily accessed by driving north on Highway 97C from Merritt or south from the town of Logan Lake. The highway, which is also called the Mamit Lake Road, is paved so an RV and car can easily reach the lake. It is the only large lake next to Highway #97C between Merritt and Logan Lake so you can't miss it.

Fishing

Despite being 165 ha in size, Mamit Lake is quite shallow with a maximum depth of only 14 m (45 ft). The lake has expansive shoals at the north and south end as well as two small islands near the south end of the lake. The shoals are easily seen, as the water is fairly clear. There is a moderately deep hole (8 m/26 ft) towards the northeastern end of the lake and the deepest area is found in the middle near the eastern shores.

Mamit Lake offers fair fishing beginning in early May for rainbow trout reaching 2 kg (5 lbs) but averaging less then 0.5 kg (1 lb). Most fishermen troll the lake with a gang troll and worm, (gold and silver) Flatfish, Lyman or Wedding Band. Trolling a muddler minnow, black leech or gomphus nymph is also productive.

Fly fishermen can do well during the spring mayfly hatch. Attractor type patterns work throughout the spring or fall.

Given the shallow depths of the lake, the fishing drops off by mid-July and the fish do not become active again until late September.

Winter fishing for burbot is very good but you have to release any you catch.

Facilities

The only developed facility at the lake is a cartop boat launch.

Lake Definition

Elevation: 970 m (3,182 ft)
Surface Area: 165 ha (408 ac)
Mean Depth: 5.5 m (18 ft)
Max Depth: 14 m (46 ft)
Perimeter: 9,150 m (30,012 ft)
Way Point: 50° 23' 00" Lat - N
120° 48' 00" Lon - W

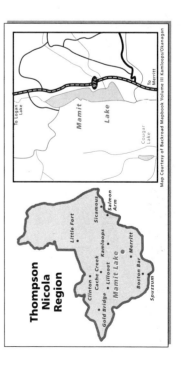

Thompson Nicola Region

Map Courtesy of Backroad Mapbook Volume III Kamloops/Okanagan

McConnell Lake

Access/Parking

McConnell Lake is easily accessed by taking the Lac Le Jeune Exit (Exit 336) on the Coquihalla Connector between Merritt and Kamloops. Head east on the paved Lac Le Jeune Road and after passing State Lake, you will see McConnell Lake on the right. For a more scenic route, travel south on the Lac Le Jeune Road from Kamloops. The road is paved so all types of vehicles can reach the lake.

Facilities

McConnell Lake is the focus of a popular recreation area given the network of X-C ski trails, biking and hiking trails. McConnell Lake Provincial Park is part of the Stake-McConnell Recreation Area and offers 15 rustic campsites, picnic facilities, pit toilets as well as a cartop boat launch.

Fishing

McConnell Lake is fairly good fishing for rainbow trout to 1 kg (2 lbs). The season extends from ice-off in early May all the way to ice-on in November. The summer doldrums do not set in because the lake is 24 m (79 ft) deep and at 1305 m (4280 ft) in elevation and the water does not warm significantly in the heat of the summer.

The lake is primarily a trolling lake with a gang troll (Willow Leaf and worm) or a Flatfish being the most popular gear. Trolling a Leech or a Doc Spratley is also a good bet.

The lake has expansive shoals towards the north and east ends of the lake. Nice drop-offs are found on both the west and east ends. Try casting a fly towards these areas using a Doc Spratley, Wooley Bugger or dragonfly nymph pattern. Chironomid, mayfly and sedge patterns are also worth a try when the hatch is on.

The water is very clear so you will be able to spot the drop-offs and shoals.

As the shores of the lake are forested, it is well advised to use a float tube or boat to fish rather than trying to cast from shore.

Other Options

Nearby **Stake Lake** offers a similar fishery. Look for the description and depth chart on page 86.

Lake Definition

Elevation:	1,305 m (4,280 ft)
Surface Area:	38 ha (95.6 ac)
Mean Depth:	8.7 m (28.5 ft)
Max Depth:	24.2 m (79.4 ft)
Perimeter:	3,460 m (11,349 ft)
Way Point:	50° 31' 25" Lat - N
	120° 28' 25" Lon - W

Recent Fish Stocking

Year	Fish Species	Life Stage	Number
1999	rainbow trout	YE	5,000
1998	rainbow trout	YE	5,000
1997	rainbow trout	YE	5,000
1996	rainbow trout	YE	5,000
1995	rainbow trout	YE	5,000

To Kamloops

ROAD

LAC LE JEUNE

McConnell Lake Rec Site

To Hwy 5 Exit 336

To Stake Lake

Anderson Cr.

Dam

2m 4 6 8m 10 12 14 16m 18 20 22 24m 4m

N

Scale

100m 0 100m 200m

Thompson Nicola Region

Little Fort
Sicamous
Salmon Arm
Cache Creek
Clinton
Kamloops
Lillooet
Gold Bridge
McConnell Lake
Merritt
Boston Bar
Spuzzum

CHEWHELS Mnt Rd
To Kamloops
McConnell Lake
LAC LE JEUNE Rd
Stake Lake
Lac Le Jeune Lake
Shambrook Lake
Walloper Lake
Exit 336
5

Map Courtesy of Backroad Mapbook Volume III Kamloops/Okanagan

McTaggart Lakes

Access/Parking

From Little Fort on Highway #5 north of Kamloops, take the ferry across the North Thompson River. Once on the east side of the river, head north on the Wildpass Road for about 4 km before the road heads sharply east. Another two kilometers and you will be at the north end of Dunn Lake. Continue south on the Dunn Lake Road to the south end of Dunn Lake. A few kilometers later you will see the McTaggart Lakes on the west side of the road.

As an alternative, longer route, you can head north on the Dunn Lake Road from Barriére. Simply follow the main road north and you will eventually reach the lakes.

Facilities

There are no developed facilities at the lakes. A resort at the south end of Dunn Lake is the closest accommodation and the Dunn Lake Rec Site at the north end of Dunn Lake is the closest developed camping area.

Fishing

McTaggart Lakes offer some reasonably good fly fishing and spincasting for rainbow trout that can reach 1 kg (2 lbs) in size. The season runs from mid-May until the early part of July. In the summer, the fishing slows down as the waters warm in the heat of the summer given the lakes are only 5-7 m (18-22 ft) deep. Try casting near the deeper parts of the lakes for better success in the summer. In late September, the fishing picks up again until the lake freezes over sometime in November.

Trolling, given the shallowness of both lakes, is hard unless you are trolling a fly or small lure right below the surface. Otherwise, you will be hooking a lot of weeds and not many fish. The lake has good insect hatches. Chironomids, sedges, damselflies, dragonflies and mayflies are later in season. Fly fishermen will have good success if they can match the hatch.

Casting a small lure such as a Deadly Dick, Flatfish or Blue Fox with a worm towards the drop-offs and shallows is also productive.

Other Options

McTaggart Lakes are found south of **Dunn Lake**. Be sure to check out page 24 for more details on the popular Dunn Lake.

Lake Definition (No. 1 Lake)

Elevation: 436 m (1,430 ft)
Surface Area: 18 ha (45.8 ac)
Mean Depth: 2.5 m (8.3 ft)
Max Depth: 5.5 m (18 ft)
Perimeter: 1930 m (6,990 ft)
Way Point: 51° 23' 00" Lat - N
120° 08' 00" Lon - W

Lake Definition (No. 2 Lake)

Elevation: 430 m (1,410 ft)
Surface Area: 17.4 m (43.1 ac)
Mean Depth: 3.4 m (11.1 ft)
Max Depth: 6.7 m (22 ft)
Perimeter: 2,240.3 m (7,350 ft)

To Little Fort

ROAD

LAKE

No. 1

5m
3
2m

Scale

100m 0 100m 200m 300m 400m 500m

N

No. 2

6
5m
3
2m

6
5m
3
2m

DUNN

To Barriere

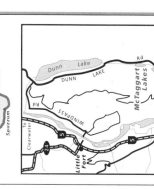

Thompson Nicola Region

Clearwater
Little Fort
McTaggart Lake
Sicamous
Salmon Arm
Clinton
Cache Creek
Kamloops
Gold Bridge
Lillooet
Merritt
Boston Bar
Spuzzum

Dunn Lake
DUNN LAKE
Rd
McTaggart Lakes
WINDPASS Rd
To Clearwater
To Kamloops
Little Fort
5
24
5

Map Courtesy of Backroad Mapbook Volume III Kamloops/Okanagan

Meadow Lake

Access/Parking

Meadow Lake is one of many pothole lakes located west of Little Fort. To reach the lake, turn left on Highway #24 at Little Fort and continue on the highway until you reach the Taweel Lake Road. Head north on this road past a series of small pothole lakes. Avoid the Blowdown Road turn-off a kilometer from the highway and then stay left. The rough road will bring you right next to the lake. It is nearby to Lost Horse and Flapjack Lakes and north of Deer Lake.

The Taweel Lake Road is a bit rough in places so a 4wd truck is a definite advantage.

Fishing

This 11 ha lake offers fair fishing for small rainbow that can reach 1.5 kg (3-4 lbs). The season begins in mid-May given its high elevation (1380 m/4365 ft) but the fishing drops off by mid-July as the summer doldrums set in. By early September, fishing begins to improve and remains active until the lake freezes over in early November.

Trolling a gang troll (Willow Leaf and worm), Flatfish or attractor type fly such as a leech is the most productive fishing method. Fly fishermen and spincasters can work the drop-off near the southeast end of the lake or the shoal at the north and west ends. The lake has most of the hatches common to the region so try to match one of them for best success.

Facilities

The Meadow Lake Fishing Camp offers rustic accommodation and a few amenities for fishermen using the lake. If you want to camp, stay at one of the rec sites at a nearby lake. The Backroad Mapbook for the Cariboo show these camping areas along with several more fishing lakes in the area.

Other Options

North of Highway 24 there are several small lakes for you to explore. The deep **Friendly Lake**, **Lost Horse Lake**, **Deer Lake** and **Laurel Lake** are a few of the better rainbow trout lakes in the area. The trout, which can reach 2 kg (5 lbs), can be taken by spin casting or fly fishing. Be sure to check out our descriptions of Laurel and Lost Horse Lakes earlier in this book.

Lake Definition

Elevation: 1,524 m (4,526 ft)
Surface Area: 7.7 ha (19 ac)
Mean Depth: 3 m (10 ft)
Max Depth: 11.3 m (37 ft)
Perimeter: 1,240.6 m (4,070 ft)
Way Point: 51° 34' 00" Lat - N
120° 24' 00" Lon - W

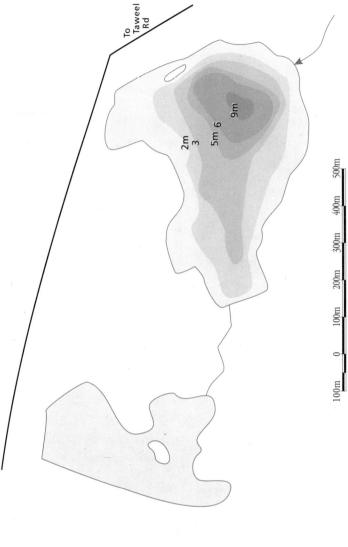

To Taweel Rd

N

2m
3
5m 6
9m

Scale

100m   0   100m   200m   300m   400m   500m

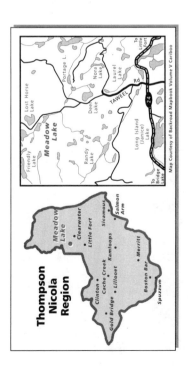

Map Courtesy of Backroad Mapbook Volume V Cariboo

Momich Lake

Access/Parking

The long drive into this lake is guaranteed to limit a lot of outdoorsmen from fishing the lake. The road to the lake, however, is very good so even a car or RV could conceivably reach the lake although it is certainly not recommended.

From the Trans Canada Highway 5.5 km northeast of Chase, take the Squilax-Anglemont Road leading north. This paved road immediately crosses a bridge over the Shuswap Lake and then heads north. Soon you will have to turn left at the first major intersection and follow the paved Holdings Road that winds gently along the western banks of the Adams River to the south end of the lake. Continue northward along the Holdings Road to the mill and from there, an excellent, well graded but windy mainhaul logging road will bring you to the north end of the Adams Lake.

From the north end of the Adams lake, take the Adams East Road in a southern direction to its junction with the Mowich-Stukemapten Forest Service Road. Drive the Mowich-Stukemapten Forest Service Road a short distance and you will soon be at the Little Momich Lake and then the main lake.

Fishing

Momich Lake is at 472 m (1,548 ft) in elevation so the ice is off fairly early in the season. It receives light fishing pressure given that the long drive into the lake discourages day trippers.

Momich Lake is a green coloured lake that is best trolled for rainbow trout and dolly varden. The fish grow to 2 kg (5 lbs) and are somewhat difficult to catch. The fishing does stay fairly steady throughout the ice-free season as the water is deep enough to ensure that it does not warm significantly in the summer months. Trollers should work the northern and southern shores of the lake using a gang troll or a lure (Krocodile, Flatfish or Kamlooper). This is because there are nice drop-offs along the shoreline.

Fly fishermen and spincasters should focus their efforts at the inflow and outflow of Momich River. Bait fishermen should also focus on those areas.

Facilities

Momich Lakes Provincial Park is a new 1648 ha park which extends up the Momich River Valley from the shores of the Adams Lake encompassing three lakes; Little Mowich Lake, Momich Lake and the Third Momich Lake. The park is open from May through October and offers camping and boat launches at several forestry recreation sites.

The Momich Lake West Rec Site is a small 2 table site with rough road access. The Momich Lake East is a much nicer site set in the cool forest next to the lake. Small trailers can be brought into the site. A sandy beach entices swimming and there is a boat launch.

Other Options

If fishing is slow in Momich Lake you may wish to try **Little Momich Lake**. Since this lake is smaller than Momich Lake fly fishing and spincasting from a float tube or from shore are much more productive than Momich Lake.

Lake Definition

Elevation:	472 m (1,548 ft)
Surface Area:	203 ha (502 ac)
Mean Depth:	34.5 m (113 ft)
Max Depth:	55 m (180 ft)
Perimeter:	8,900 m (29,192 ft)
Way Point:	51° 19' 00" Lat - N
	119° 21' 00" Lon - W

Thompson Nicola Region

Map Courtesy of Backroad Mapbook Volume III Kamloops/Okanagan

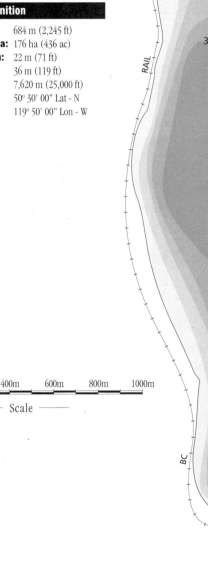

To Kamloops

MONTE   LAKE   FSR

97

N

8m
15

22m

30

RAIL

30m

22

15

8

BC

Monte Lake
Provincial
Park

97

Pringle   Cr

To
Vernon

Access/Parking

Monte Lake is found right next to Highway #97 northwest of Westwold and west of Falkland. The highway passes by the eastern shores of the lake so it would be hard to miss.

To reach Highway #97, drive north of Vernon or east of Kamloops on the Trans Canada Highway.

Fishing

Monte Lake is not a great fishing destination lake but we included it in this book because of the easy access and the fact it is a nice lake to fish. The lake offers fair fishing for rainbow trout to 2 kg (4-5 lbs). Unfortunately, there are too many course fish in the lake which are out competing the rainbow for the available food source. The lake is most suited to trolling beginning in early May. Try a gang troll or a small lure such as a Panther Martin, Flatfish, Krokodile or Kamlooper. Trolling a leech, muddler minnow or Doc Spratley is also a good idea.

Fly fishermen should focus their effort around the outflow creek towards the south end of lake. The lake also has distinctive drop-offs around its entire length which can be fished. There are few shoals to work, however.

Facilities

Monte Lake Provincial Park is on the eastern shores of the lake. The park provides 10 camping spots and is fairly popular in the summer months. The nice picnic facilities and the beach are the main attractions to the park. A private campground acts as an overflow when the provincial park is full.

Other Options

Biancotto Lake and **Paxton Lake** are two small lakes located east of Monte Lake. The lakes are found off the Paxton Valley Road and offer fly fishing and spincasting.

Lake Definition

Elevation:	684 m (2,245 ft)
Surface Area:	176 ha (436 ac)
Mean Depth:	22 m (71 ft)
Max Depth:	36 m (119 ft)
Perimeter:	7,620 m (25,000 ft)
Way Point:	50° 30' 00" Lat - N
	119° 50' 00" Lon - W

100m   0   200m   400m   600m   800m   1000m

——— Scale ———

Recent Fish Stocking

Year	Fish Species	Life Stage	Number
1999	rainbow trout	YE	20,000
1998	rainbow trout	YE	20,000
1997	rainbow trout	YE	20,000
1996	rainbow trout	YE	20,000
1995	rainbow trout	YE	18,500

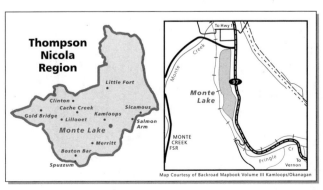

Map Courtesy of Backroad Mapbook Volume III Kamloops/Okanagan

Mowich Lake

Access/Parking

At the east end of Kamloops Lake, the Trans Canada Highway crosses the Thompson River on an impressive bridge. Head north from the bridge and you will soon cross the Deadman River. The Deadman-Vidette Road leads directly north from the west side of the Deadman River Bridge. Stay on the main logging road avoiding any detours. The first lake you will reach is Mowich Lake, which will be on the west side of the road.

Fishing

Mowich Lake has reasonably good fishing for rainbow and kokanee that reach 1 kg (2 lbs) in size. The lake is only 14.5 m (45 ft) deep, which restricts trolling somewhat. Nice fertile shoals are located near the north and south ends of the lake. Productive drop-offs are found around the entire lake.

Trollers should use a Willow Leaf and worm or maggot for both the rainbow and kokanee. Some of the smaller lures such as a Flatfish, Panther Martin or Deadly Dick also work for the rainbow. Pink lures such as the spin-n-glow and Dick Nite take kokanee.

Fly fishermen should focus their efforts around the shoals at the north end or the drop-offs around the rest of the lake. Most of the insect hatches common to the region are also found at this lake so try matching one of the hatches.

It is possible to fish from shore as the lake drops off rapidly but a float tube or boat is definitely a real benefit. The lake, given its elevation and depth, has a reasonably good fishery during the summer months.

Facilities

There is a fine resort at the north end of the lake but no developed camping sites.

Other Options

Hudson Bay Lake is a short drive away from Mowich Lake. From the south end of Mowich Lake, head northwest on the Clinton-Brigade Road and the lake will appear on the left.

Continuing north on the Deadman Vidette Road, you will find **Snohoosh**, **Skookum**, **Deadmans** and **Vidette Lakes**. These lakes are all highlighted in this book.

Lake Definition

Elevation:	746.8 m (2,450 ft)
Surface Area:	28.6 ha (70.7 ac)
Mean Depth:	9.4 m (30.8 ft)
Max Depth:	14.6 m (48 ft)
Perimeter:	2,927 m (9,600 ft)
Way Point:	50° 02' 00" Lat - N
	120° 54' 00" Lon - W

Scale
100m 0 200m 400m 600m

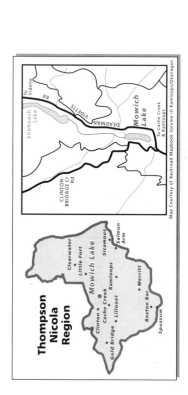

Map Courtesy of Backroad Mapbook Volume III Kamloops/Okanagan

Thompson Nicola Region

Murray Lake

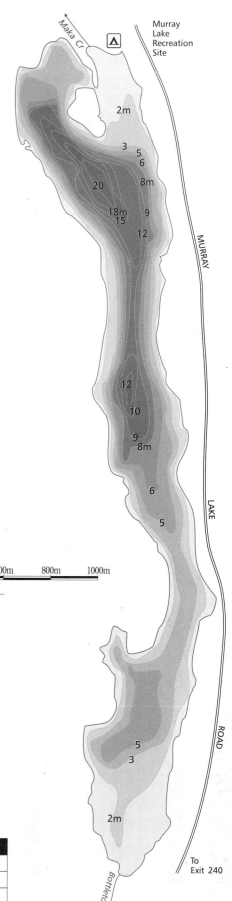

Access/Parking

Murray Lake is accessed by taking the third exit (Juliet-Exit 240) north of the Coquihalla Highway toll booth. Head north on the Murray Lake Road from the highway and within 4 km you will see the long, narrow lake on your left.

Fishing

Despite the easy access, Murray Lake is still known as a great fishing lake. The preferred methods of fishing are trolling and fly fishing beginning in mid-May and running to late October. The summer doldrums are not a problem at the lake given that the lake is fairly high in elevation.

Trollers focus on a gang troll but can do well trolling an attractor type fly such as a leech, Carey Special or Doc Spratley. Small lures like a Panther Martin or Flatfish are effective at times.

Fly fishermen should work the shoals and drop-offs with a dragonfly nymph, leech or shrimp patterns. Other attractor type patterns such as a Doc Spratley or muddler minnow are worth a try.

Facilities

Murray Lake has two forest service rec sites with a total of 14 camping spots. Cartop boat launches are found at the rec sites as well.

Other Options

In the Murray Lake area, there are three other lesser known lakes that may be worth a try if the fish are not biting at Murray lake. All three lakes (**Debbie Lake**, **Jono Lake** and **Michael Lake**) are best accessed by travelling past the north end of Murray Lake and taking the Debbie Lake Forest Service Road at the 22.5 km mark. Michael Lake involves a hike whereas both Debbie Lake and Jono Lake are located on spur roads off the Debbie Lake Road. All three lakes are small and suited to fly fishing or spincasting from a float tube. The lakes are reported to hold descent numbers of small rainbow.

Lake Definition

Surface Area: 35 ha
Way Point: 49° 29' 00" Lat - N
115° 20' 00" Lon - W

N

200m   0   200m   400m   600m   800m   1000m

——— Scale ———

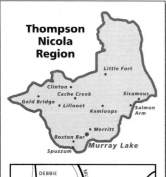

Thompson Nicola Region

Little Fort
Clinton
Cache Creek
Sicamous
Gold Bridge Lillooet
Kamloops
Salmon Arm
Boston Bar Merritt
Spuzzum **Murray Lake**

DEBBIE LAKE FSR
Murray Lake
Debbie Lake
Jono Lake
COLDWATER Rd
COQUIHALLA Hwy
5
To Hope

Recent Fish Stocking

Year	Fish Species	Life Stage	Number
1998	rainbow trout	FF	5,000
1997	rainbow trout	FR	5,000
1996	rainbow trout	FF	5,000
1995	rainbow trout	FF	5,000

Nicola Lake

Access/Parking

Nicola Lake is the large, deep lake 22 km northeast of Merritt. The lake can be seen from the Coquihalla Highway when you are heading north towards Kamloops. The lake is set in a dry, open landscape where trees are a rarity. To reach the lake, head northeast on Highway #5A from Merritt.

Fishing

Nicola Lake offers a wide variety of fish and the fishery remains active throughout the year. Although 9 kg (20 lb) trout have been pulled out of the lake, small kokanee to 0.5 kg (1 lb) and rainbow trout to 2 kg (4-5 lbs) are more common. The lake receives fairly light fishing pressure considering the easy access. The lake begins to warm in the summer months so the rainbow retreat to the depths. You can still catch the rainbow so long as you fish at the 9-18 m (30-60 ft) level.

Trolling is the mainstay of the lake but be wary of strong winds. Roostertails, Mepps, Flatfish, wedding bands, Lyman, Dick Nite, Kwikfish and a Spin 'n Glow all work for both the kokanee and rainbow. Rainbow fishermen should not rule out Panther Martins or Flatfish, especially in the spring and fall. A Willow Leaf with bait (maggots or worm) trolled slowly during June to mid-July is the most effective for the kokanee. Keep the gear at the 3-6 m (10-20 ft) level.

In the winter, burbot fishing is good but the fish must be released.

Facilities

The lake is more of a summer recreation and watersport lake then a fishing lake. It has a variety of facilities lining the lake from private residences to campgrounds and boat launches.

Monck Provincial Park is found on the northern shores of Nicola Lake and is easily accessed by the Monck Park Road. It is an extremely popular park which is open from March to November and contains 71 camping spots as well as a large (130 table) picnic area. There are full facilities at the park as well as swimming, fishing, hiking and paddling opportunities. If you have time, be sure to hike to the lava beds or explore the historical native areas.

Other Options

Other large lakes within close proximity to Nicola Lake include **Stump Lake** (which is described on page 88) and **Douglas Lake**. Douglas Lake is 650 ha and offers rainbow and small kokanee, primarily by trolling.

Lake Definition

Elevation:	623 m (2,045 ft)
Surface Area:	6,215 ha (15,358 ac)
Mean Depth:	23 m (77 ft)
Max Depth:	57 m (187 ft)
Perimeter:	50° 10' 00" Lat - N
Way Point:	120° 32' 00" Lon - W

Thompson Nicola Region

Little Fort
Sicamous
Salmon Arm
Clinton
Cache Creek
Kamloops
Gold Bridge
Lillooet
Nicola Lake
Boston Bar
Merritt
Spuzzum

To Stump Lake
5A
Nicola Lake
Quilchena
Nicola
Merritt
5
9

Map Courtesy of Backroad Mapbook Volume III Kamloops/Okanagan

To Slump Lake

Stump Lake Cr
Moore Cr

Nicola Lake Indian Reserve

Nicola River

Quilchena

PENNASK LAKE Rd

Quilchena Cr

IR

Monck Provincial Park

Rd

PARK

MONCK

Nicola R.

To Merritt

Nicola

N

Scale

500m   0   1km   2km   3km   4km

Access/Parking

From Kamloops, head northeast on the Trans Canada Highway to Pritchard. Take the bridge over the South Thompson River and hang a right on the Shuswap Road. Within 7 km, the Niskonlith Lake Road heads north. Follow that road for a few kilometers and you will reach the south end of the lake.

From Chase, take the Shuswap Road past Little Shuswap Lake and across the South Thompson River. Soon you will be heading south and the Loakin-Bear Creek Road will appear as the first major intersection on the right. Drive the Loakin-Bear Creek Road and after a few switchbacks, you will be at the Niskonlith Lake Road junction. Take that road and within 2 km you will be at the north end of the lake.

Regardless of your approach to the lake, the access is along good gravel roads.

Fishing

Niskonlith Lake is mainly a trolling lake with a season that runs from May to November. Despite its location, the lake receives light fishing pressure allowing for consistent fishing for rainbow in the 1 kg (1-2 lb) range and kokanee up to 0.5 kg (1 lb).

Trollers do well catching rainbow with a weeding band, Flatfish or small spinner. A Willow Leaf with a maggot trolled slowly is your best bet for the kokanee.

Recent Fish Stocking

Year	Fish Species	Life Stage	Number
1997	rainbow trout, kokanee	YE, FR	68,060
1996	rainbow trout, kokanee	YE, FR	70,050
1995	rainbow trout, kokanee	YE, FR	45,000

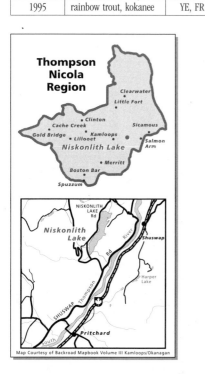

Thompson Nicola Region

Map Courtesy of Backroad Mapbook Volume III Kamloops/Okanagan

For fly fishermen, try an attractor type pattern like a Doc Spratley or a woolly bugger. Also, good hatches are offered in the spring and summer with the best place to fish being around the island near the northeast end of the lake. The large shoal area at the north and south ends of the lake are also worth a try.

There is an engine power restriction (no motors over 10 hp) on the lake.

Facilities

Niskonlith Lake Provincial Park is a small park with 30 campsites located on the eastern shores of the lake. Although there is no developed boat launch, it is still possible to launch cartoppers.

Lake Definition

Elevation:	513 m (1,684 ft)
Surface Area:	370 ha (914 ac)
Mean Depth:	18.6 m (61 ft)
Max Depth:	36.6 m (120 ft)
Perimeter:	11,888 m (39,000 ft)
Way Point:	50° 47' 00" Lat - N
	119° 46' 00" Lon - W

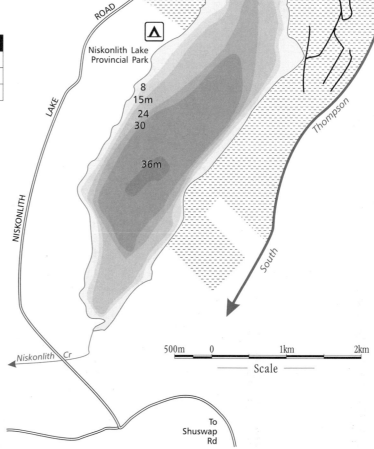

Noble Lake

Access/Parking

Noble Lake is located just north of the Lac Du Bois Grasslands Provincial Park, which, in turn, is found north of Kamloops and west of the North Thompson River. The lake can be reached by one of two ways. Take the Lac Du Bois Road north from Kamloops to the 15 km mark. Hang a right and you will soon pass by McQueen Lake and Griffin Lake. Keep left at the intersection just east of Griffin Lake and you will then pass by Isobel Lake. Within a kilometer of Isobel Lake, a 4wd side road heads north and leads to Noble Lake.

The second route is to head north on the Westsyde Road north of Kamloops and after leaving the Lac Du Bois Grasslands Provincial Park, take the Cannel Road heading west. After switchbacking out of the North Thompson River Valley, turn left on the first major intersection and stay right. You will soon reach the 4wd spur road heading north to Noble Lake. If you reach Isobel Lake you have gone too far.

Fishing

Noble Lake is a small (8 ha) lake, which is created by a dam at the south end of the lake. The lake has a long, narrow bay at the north end, which is very shallow and full of aquatic vegetation. Sharp drop-offs are located on both the western and eastern shores of the lake with the water dropping off to over 18 m (60 ft).

Noble Lake has fairly good fishing for rainbow that can reach 1+kg (2 lbs) in size but average 20-30 cm (8-12"). The fishing begins in mid-May with a number of good insect hatches through to the early part of July. For fly fishermen, try a dragonfly nymph cast near the weeds or try matching the mayfly or chirono-mid hatches. As the water is clear, the fly presentation should be made on a long, fine leader to avoid spooking the fish with the fly line.

Trolling the lake is possible as long as you work a tight circle near the middle of the lake. Otherwise, the gear will be dragged through weeds. Try a small lure such as a Flatfish or Mepps, a gang troll or an attractor type fly such as a wooley bugger or Doc Spratley.

The summer doldrums set in by mid-July and so the lake isn't worth fishing until late September. Into October, you can do very well as the fish are storing up energy for the long winter. Some of the larger fish are taken at that time.

Facilities

Other than a rough cartop boat launch, there are no developed facilities at the lake.

Other Options

Nearby to **Noble Lake** are **Isobel Lake**, **Griffin Lake**, **McQueen Lake** and **Pass Lake**. All the lakes provide decent trout fishing.

Lake Definition

Elevation:	1,067 m (3,500 ft)
Surface Area:	8 ha (20 ac)
Mean Depth:	8.8 m (29 ft)
Max Depth:	20 m (66 ft)
Perimeter:	1,609.4 m (5,280 ft)
Way Point:	50º 52' 00" Lat - N
	120º 23' 00" Lon - W

Recent Fish Stocking

Year	Fish Species	Life Stage	Number
1998	rainbow trout	FF	2,000
1997	rainbow trout	FF	2,000
1996	rainbow trout	FF	4,000
1995	rainbow trout	FF	4,000

Scale
100m 0 100m 200m 300m 400m 500m

N

Dam

6
9m
12
15m
18

Thompson Nicola Region

Little Fort
Clinton
Cache Creek
Gold Bridge
Lillooet
Kamloops
Noble Lake
Sicamous
Salmon Arm
Merritt
Boston Bar
Spuzzum

O Connor Lake
Creek
CANNEL Rd
WESTSYDE Rd
Lanes
Noble Lake
Isobel Lake
Griffin Lake
McQUEEN LAKE FSR

Map Courtesy of Backroad Mapbook Volume III Kamloops/Okanagan

North Barriére Lake

Access/Parking

North Barriére Lake is located to the west of Adams Lake and east of Barriére. Head north on Highway #5 from Kamloops to Barriére where you will find the Barriére Lakes Road. This paved road heads east up the Barriére River Valley. After about 17.5 km you will come to a three way intersection. Take a left heading north along the North Barriére Lake Forest Service Road. The road will soon lead along the northern shores of the lake.

Fishing

North Barriére Lake is a deep (maximum 52.5 m/175 ft), cold lake, which does not receive a lot of fishing pressure. The lake contains large dollies (to 5 kg/12 lbs), rainbow (to 2 kg/5 lbs) and lake trout (to 4 kg/ 10 lbs). There are also some smaller kokanee, whitefish and burbot.

Fishing is generally slow from ice-off in early May to when the lake freezes over in November. However, dollies, rainbow or lake trout caught at this time are likely to be big.

The preferred method of fishing is trolling. For the lake trout and dollies try a plug or spoon such as an Apex, Krokodile or large Flatfish. Earlier in the spring and late in the fall, you can fish near the surface in 3-6 m (10-20ft) of water focusing on the steep drop-off areas at the north and south ends of the lake. As the summer approaches, the fish move into the depths so try at the 9-25 m (30-90 ft) level.

Both the rainbow and the kokanee take a Willow Leaf and worm. Rainbows also strike small lures such as a wedding band, Flatfish or Mepps. Try trolling an attractor type fly for the rainbow like a leech or Doc Spratley.

Fly fishermen will be a little disappointed with this lake. They should focus their efforts at the outflow to the Barriére River located at the west end of the lake. The shallows at the east end also look fairly inviting as does the estuary of Vermelin Creek.

In terms of fly patterns to use, fly fishermen should try a chironomid pupae, mayfly nymph or damselfly nymph.

Facilities

There is a rec site on the north side of the lake offering camping as well as launching facilities.

The North Barriére Lake Resort (250-376-9922) has 7 rustic cabins for a reasonable fee together with 35 campsites including some with hook-ups. Flush toilets, showers, boat rentals and a sani-station are some of the other features of the resort.

Other Options

East Barriére, Saskum and South Barriére Lakes are all found in the area. East Barriére and Saskum Lake are described in this book. South Barriére Lake also offers good fishing for rainbow in the spring and fall.

Lake Definition

Elevation:	637 m (2,090 ft)
Surface Area:	453.8 ha (1,121 ac)
Mean Depth:	24.7 m (81 ft)
Max Depth:	52.6 m (173 ft)
Perimeter:	5,334.1 m (57,400 ft)
Way Point:	51° 20' 00" Lat - N
	119° 50' 00" Lon -

Map Courtesy of Backroad Mapbooks Volume III Kamloops/Okanagan

Paradise Lake

Access/Parking

Paradise Lake is one of 13 lakes located in an area north of the Elkhart Exit on the Okanagan Connector. After exiting the highway, head north on the Elkhart Road and hang a right at the north end of Bob's Lake. Island Lake will soon appear on the left side of the road within a few hundred meters followed by Paradise Lake on the right side.

Fishing

Paradise Lake is a good family fishing lake as it has many small rainbow trout easily caught by fly fishing or trolling. The odd rainbow grows to 2 kg (4-5 lbs).

The lake is comprised of dark, nutrient rich water ideal for insects and aquatic vertebrae. The lake is only 11.9 m (39 ft) deep and has some nice shallows near the south end. As a result of the depth and the water warming in the summer, the summer lag hits the lake with a vengeance.

Trolling the lake in the spring and fall is common. The gear of choice is small lures, a Flatfish or a gang troll. Trolling an attractor type fly pattern such as a leech or Doc Spratley should be considered.

Fly fishermen can do well casting a damselfly or dragonfly nymph near the shallows at the south end. The usual insect hatches occur at the lake so try matching the hatch.

Due to the abundance of small trout, you can keep up to 8 daily.

Facilities

The lake has a cartop boat launch as well as a resort. The resort, located at the northwest end of the lake, has meals, boat rentals and cabins. The closest forest service rec site is at Island Lake.

Other Options

Johns Lake, Skunk Lake, Bob's Lake, Elkhart Lake, Boot Lake and **Reservoir Lake** are all in the vicinity. The Backroad Mapbook for the Kamloops/Okanagan shows you how to find all of these lakes and what kind of fishing you can expect.

Lake Definition

Elevation: 1,524 m (5,000 ft)
Surface Area: 135.6 ha (335 ac)
Mean Depth: 5.2 m (17 ft)
Max Depth: 11.9 m (39 ft)
Perimeter: 5,364.5 m (17,600 ft)
Way Point: 49° 55' 00" Lat - N
120° 17' 00" Lon - W

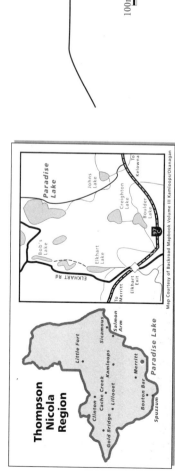

Thompson Nicola Region

Clinton · Little Fort · Sicamous · Salmon Arm · Cache Creek · Kamloops · Gold Bridge · Lillooet · Merritt · Boston Bar · Spuzzum · Paradise Lake

Paradise Lake · Johns Lake · Creighton Lake · Boulder Lake · Bob's Lake · Elkhart Lake · ELKHART RD · Elkhart Exit · To Merritt · To Kelowna · 97C

Map Courtesy of Backroad Mapbook Volume III Kamloops/Okanagan

Quilchena Cr

Mount Ford's Camp

resort

ROAD

LAKE

PARADISE

To Hwy 97C

To John Lake

1m

2

3

4m

4m

N

Scale

100m 0 100m 200m 300m 400m 500m

Pass Lake

Access/Parking

Pass Lake is best reached by driving 20 km northwest of Kamloops on the Lac Du Bois Road. This road brings you through the heart of the new Lac Du Bois Grasslands Provincial Park. After leaving the park and passing by Lac Du Bois take a left at the 15 km mark. Within 3 km, Pass Lake will appear on the north side of the road.

In dry weather, it is possible to bring a car to the lake but a truck is highly recommended. After a good rain or in early spring, a truck is required.

Fishing

Pass Lake is a small, unassuming lake yet it hold some big Kamloops trout which can reach 3 kg (6-8 lbs). The fish, however, are notoriously hard to catch even for the best fly fishermen. The fishing begins around May 1 after the ice is gone and continues into early November with the summer being fairly slow. The lake receives a fair bit of fishing pressure but because it is a fly fishing only lake, the stock is being maintained. Also, to maintain the stock, there is a daily limit of one trout over 50 cm (none under), a bait ban, a single barbless hook restriction and an ice fishing closure.

The lake is best fished in the early season or again in late September to October. A float tube, canoe or rowboat will be a definite advantage. The lake drops off rapidly to just over 13 m (40 ft) providing some nice drop-offs to sample. Small shoal areas with weeds are found at the west and north ends of the lake. Since the water is clear, the drop-offs and shoals can be pinpointed from your boat.

The best hatch to fish is the early spring chironomid. In 6 m (20+ ft) of water, sink a size #12-16 black, brown or olive green chironomid pupa pattern to the bottom and retrieve it very slowly is very effective. A floating line with a 6 m (20 ft) leader is the easiest way to get the fly to the bottom and imitate an emerging chironomid adult.

Later in the spring or into the fall, try casting a damselfly or dragonfly nymph towards the weeds at the west end of the lake. Leech, sedge, and caddisfly patterns work well in the spring and fall. Try casting near the drop-offs.

Facilities

A rec site offers a nice place to camp and launch a small boat. There are a total of 15 vehicle units at the rec site.

Other Options

Pass Lake is close to **McQueen Lake**, **Griffin Lake**, **Isobel Lake** and **Lac du Bois**.

Lake Definition

Elevation:	948 m (3,110 ft)
Surface Area:	28 ha (69 ac)
Mean Depth:	7.3 m (24 ft)
Max Depth:	13 m (42 ft)
Perimeter:	2,414 m (7,920 ft)
Way Point:	50° 50' 00" Lat - N
	120° 29' 00" Lon - W

Recent Fish Stocking

Year	Fish Species	Life Stage	Number
1997	rainbow trout	YE	2,500
1996	rainbow trout	YE	2,500
1995	rainbow trout	YE	2,500

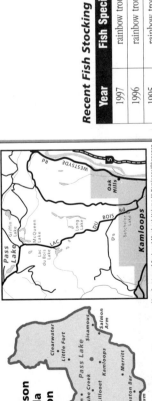

Map Courtesy of Backroad Mapbook Volume III Kamloops/Okanagan

Thompson Nicola Region

Paul Lake

Access/Parking

This popular lake is located 17 km east of Highway #5 on a paved road (Paul Lake Road). To find the lake, cross the South Thompson River Bridge on Highway #5 and take the Paul lake Road turn-off after travelling several kilometers.

Fishing

Paul Lake is infested with red-sided shiners first introduced to the lake by bait fishermen. The course fish have taken their toll on the rainbow stock by out competing them. However, there can still be descent fishing in the early spring and late fall due to the annual stocking program. In fact, many consider this lake as one of the best fly fishing lakes in May. The rainbow are generally pan size but some can reach 2.5 kg (5 lbs) on occasion.

Trolling is by far the most popular fishing method. A gang troll, Flatfish or flies (leech, muddler minnow or other minnow patterns) are the gear of choice. You will need a boat and motor to cover the lake.

Fly fishermen seek out Paul Lake for the prolific dry-fly fishing during the sedge hatch in late June-early July. Early in the year, a chironomid pupa pattern sunk past the drop-offs and retrieved slowly from the bottom is effective. Cast a mayfly imitation in late May-early June near the shoals at the north end of the lake. A damselfly or dragonfly nymph cast towards the weedbeds also produces. In August, a minnow pattern is the best bet.

In the summer months, the lake warms and fly fishing is very unproductive. Switching to a deep troll will improve the chances of success.

Facilities

The Paul Lake Provincial Park is open from April to October and provides 111 camping spots as well as a huge picnic area, a boat launch, playground and sani-station. The multi-use park is very popular during the summer since it has 7 km of hiking trails as well as plenty of water sport activities.

Other Options

Louis Lake and **Pinantan Lake** can be easily reached along the Pinantan-Pritchard Road. These rural lakes do offer rainbow fishing, primarily by trolling. Please be careful of private property in the area.

Lake Definition

Surface Area:	258 ha (638 ac)
Mean Depth:	29 m (94.8 ft)
Max Depth:	55 m (181 ft)
Perimeter:	12,344.5 m (40,500 ft)
Way Point:	50° 44' 00" Lat - N
	120° 07' 00" Lon - W

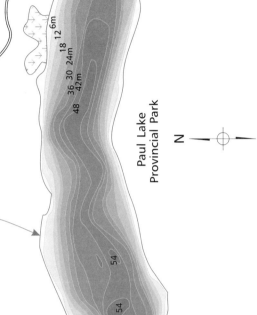

PINATAN-

PRITCHARD ROAD

Lloyd Cr

Paul Lake Provincial Park

Paul Lake Provincial Park

LAKE ROAD

PAUL

Paul Cr

N

500m   0   1km   2km

Scale

Recent Fish Stocking

Year	Fish Species	Life Stage	Number
1997	rainbow trout	YE	40,050
1996	rainbow trout	YE	25,000
1995	rainbow trout	YE	18,025

Map Courtesy of Backroad Mapbook Volume III Kamloops/Okanagan

Thompson Nicola Region

Clearwater
Little Fort
Sicamous
Salmon Arm
Kamloops
Clinton
Cache Creek
Lilloet
Paul Lake
Merritt
Gold Bridge
Boston Bar
Spuzzum

Pavilion Lake

Access/Parking

Pavilion Lake is located east of the tiny Native Indian community of Pavilion on Highway #99. Take Highway #99 north from Lillooet winding along the east banks of the Fraser River until you reach Pavilion. Continue along the highway from Pavilion until you reach the northwest end of Pavilion Lake.

Alternatively, drive Highway #97 to Cache Creek. Head north from Cache Creek until you reach the junction with Highway #99. Take Highway #99 in the westward direction until you reach the southeast end of the lake.

Fishing

Pavilion is not a very productive lake as compared to some of the Thompson/Nicola Region lakes. It still is worth a try if you are in the Lillooet area and want to stop over at a scenic provincial park for some camping and fishing.

Pavilion Lake has fair fishing for rainbow to 1.5 kg primarily by trolling a gang troll with a wedding ring and worm or a Flatfish. Fly fishermen will generally be disappointed with the lake. Try casting an attractor type fly near one of the creek estuaries or at the outflow at the northwest end of the lake.

There is also an ice fishing season at the lake, which begins in late December and runs until March.

Facilities

Sky Blue Water Resort (250-256-7633) is found on the shores of Pavilion Lake. There is rustic cabins, campsites and picnic area, boat rentals and a concession & snack bar.

At the southeast end of the lake is the Marble Canyon Provincial Park. It also encompasses Turquoise and Crown Lakes, two small scenic lakes set at the base of 1000 m (3300 ft) high limestone cliffs. There are a total of 34 campsites between the lakes. Picnicking, swimming, fishing and hiking are the primary attractions to the park.

Other Options

Crown Lake is an 18 ha lake found to the southeast. It has rainbow to 1 kg (2 lbs) best caught by fly fishing or casting a small lure throughout the spring or fall. There is a cartop boat launch at the lake.

Turquoise Lake has good fishing for stocked rainbow growing to 1 kg (2 lbs) primarily by casting a small lure or by fly fishing. The 10 ha lake is also found southeasr of Pavillion Lake. A cartop boat launch is available at the lake.

Lake Definition

Elevation: 610 m (2,000 ft)
Surface Area: 262 ha (647 ac)
Mean Depth: 25 m (83 ft)
Max Depth: 56 m (184 ft)
Perimeter: 14,215 m (46,636 ft)
Way Point: 50° 52' 00" Lat - N
121° 44' 00" Lon - W

Recent Fish Stocking

Year	Fish Species	Life Stage	Number
1997	rainbow trout	YE	40,000
1996	rainbow trout	YE	40,000
1995	rainbow trout	YE	40,000

Map Courtesy of Backroad Mapbook Volume III Kamloops/Okanagan

70

Pennask Lake

Access/Parking

To reach the lake, leave the Okanagan Connector at the Sunset Exit and drive to the south of the connector. Then, travel 6 km east right next to the highway. At the 6 km mark, a major intersection will appear. Travel a very short distance south on the Sunset Lake Forest Service Road (FSR) and you will see the Bear Creek FSR heading off to the left. Take that road under the Okanagan Connector and you are on your way to the lake.

While travelling northeast on the Bear Creek Forest Service Road, take the second or third intersection to the left. The first of the roads, (at 13.2 km on the Bear Creek FSR), leads to the west side of the lake, whereas the second of the roads leads to the east side of the lake and the provincial park. Unfortunately, the access roads into the lake are very rough and a 4wd truck is well advised. You can reach the lake by 2wd truck though.

Jackson Lake is best reached by taking a boat to the north end of Pennask Lake and walking 1 km along the Pennask Lake Trail. The trail network can also be reached by travelling on a spur road leading from the Pennask Lake FSR.

Fishing

Pennask Lake is a large (965 ha) lake with a fly only restriction. There are many rainbow in the 0.5-1 kg (1-2 lb) range making this lake one of the most consistent producers in the region. In fact, rainbow spawning in the inlet creek provides 30% of all the eggs for the provincial hatchery program. This isn't surprising considering the lake is said to have the largest run of spawning, wild rainbow in Canada, if not the world.

The fishing season runs from mid-May to early November and remains active all summer. Despite the fast action, the lake only receives moderate fishing pressure probably because of the artificial fly only restriction, bait ban, ice fishing ban and single barbless hook restriction.

The most consistent fly patterns seem to be shrimp or mayfly imitations or a #12 Black Doc Spratley. Since the fish are plentiful, just about any fly in your tackle box works.

The lake is subject to strong winds and some summer thunderstorms so always be weary of the weather.

Jackson Lake offers good fishing for rainbow to 2 kg (4-5 lbs). Fishing remains active from May to November. In the spring and fall, focus on the shoals and drop-offs. As summer approaches, try around the deep hole. Jackson Lake also has strict regulations in place.

Facilities

Pennask Lake Provincial Park is a year round provincial park located on the southeast shore of Pennask Lake off the Pennask FSR (rough 2wd access). The provincial park has 28 rustic camp spots together with a boat launch, a day use area and some pit toilets.

Lake Definition (Pennask Lake)

Elevation:	1,402 m (4,600 ft)
Surface Area:	1,041 ha (2,573 ac)
Mean Depth:	20 m (6.1 ft)
Max Depth:	50 m (15.2 ft)
Perimeter:	24,549 m (80,520 ft)
Way Point:	50° 10' 00" Lat - N
	120° 32' 00" Lon - W

Recent Fish Stocking

Year	Fish Species	Life Stage	Number
1998	rainbow trout	FF	2,000
1996	rainbow trout	FF	2,000

Thompson Nicola Region

Access/Parking

Peter Hope Lake is found northwest of Douglas Lake and northeast of Nicola Lake in cattle country. To reach the lake, begin on Highway 5A from either Kamloops or Merritt and near the south end of Stump Lake, you will find the Peterhope Road leading east. Drive east on the road and stay on the main road all the way to the north end of the lake.

An alternative route is to take the Douglas Lake Road, which begins near the north end of Nicola Lake on Highway #5A. At the 7 km mark, follow the Lauder Road leading northeast. Continue on the Lauder Road past Glimpse Lake to the 17.5 km mark and then hang a left. This road will take you to the south end of Peter Hope Lake.

Fishing

Peter Hope Lake is a man-made lake dammed in the 1930's for irrigation purposes. In 1942, the lake was stocked with rainbow and has been a consistent producer of large Kamloops trout ever since.

Peter Hope Lake has deep, clear water surrounded by extensive marl flats ideal for insect life. The shoreline is reed covered and there are two submerged islands with deep channels between them, making this an ideal fly fishing lake.

The lake is known to have some very large Kamloops trout exceeding 9 kg (20 lbs) but they are tough to catch. The average fish is under 2 kg (4-5 lbs) and if you get one in the 3 kg (6-7 lbs) range you will get the bragging rights for the weekend.

Beginning after ice off in early May, the rainbow are seen cruising the extensive flats so you should focus on the fringe area between the flats and the deep water. Chironomids pupae work all season on a sinking line retrieved slowly from the depths (less than 6 m/20 ft). Mayfly, dragonfly nymphs and damselfly nymphs produce beginning in June. Caddisfly patterns are productive in late June-early July.

Facilities

There is a rec site at the north end of the lake. It has 15 camping sites together with a cartop boat launch.

The Peter Hope Lodge (250-371-7330) has rustic accommodation as well as a public campground.

In the summer months, the fish retreat to the depths. Weighted dragonfly nymphs or chironomid papa patterns on a fast sinking line cast at the edge of the shoals is very productive.

By mid-September to late October, the fish begin cruising the flats again and you should move back to the fringes. Bead-head leech and woolly bugger patterns work well.

The lake is closed for ice fishing, has a bait ban, requires a single barbless hook and has a daily limit of 2 rainbow.

Lake Definition

Elevation:	1,112.5 m (3,650 ft)
Surface Area:	116 ha (287 ac)
Mean Depth:	11.5 m (38 ft)
Max Depth:	32.9 m (108 ft)
Perimeter:	3,324 m (10,906 ft)
Way Point:	50° 18' 00" Lat - N
	120° 19' 00" Lon - W

Peterhope Lake Rec Site

PETERHOPE

Peterhope Cr

Peterhope Cr

39m

15

21m

27

30m

ROAD

N

Recent Fish Stocking

Year	Fish Species	Life Stage	Number
1997	rainbow trout	YE	12,000
1996	rainbow trout	YE	12,000
1995	rainbow trout	YE	12,000

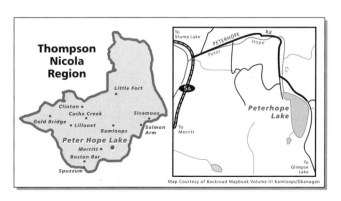

Thompson Nicola Region

Little Fort

Clinton • Cache Creek
Gold Bridge • Lillooet Sicamous •
  Kamloops Salmon Arm
Peter Hope Lake
  Merritt •
Boston Bar •
Spuzzum •

To Stump Lake PETERHOPE Rd
Peter Hope
5A
To Merritt
Peterhope Lake
Cr
To Glimpse Lake

Map Courtesy of Backroad Mapbook Volume III Kamloops/Okanagan

200m   0   200m   400m   600m   800m   1000m

—— Scale ——

Pinantan Lake

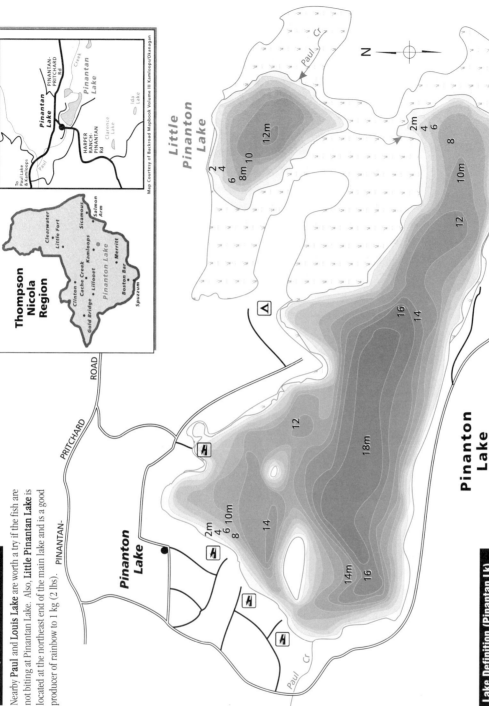

Map Courtesy of Backroad Mapbook Volume III Kamloops/Okanagan

Access/Parking

Pinantan Lake is easily accessed by RVs or cars as it is found 24 km from Highway #5 on a paved road.

To reach the lake, cross the South Thompson River Bridge on Highway #5 and taking the Paul lake Road turn-off after travelling 5 km northward on Highway #5. Just before reaching Paul Lake, take the Pinantan-Pritchard Road to the left, which leads around the north side of both Louis and Paul Lake. Stay on the main road for 13 km and you will soon come to Pinantan Lake.

Fishing

The lake is fairly good for fishing for rainbow that can reach 2 kg (4-5 lbs) although the average is 20-25 cm (8-10"). The fishing probably would be better if it were not for the red sided shiner problem and the fact those coarse fish out compete the rainbow for the available food.

The lake has clear water with weed covered shorelines. The fishing begins in mid-April and sees a lull in mid-July to late September. By the middle of November, the lake is frozen over.

Trolling is the mainstay of the lake with gang trolls and a Flatfish being very popular. Fly fishing, although generally spotty throughout the year, is best in the early spring when using a Mayfly pattern or attractor type patterns. In the summer, try using a dry fly like a mosquito, Grizzly King or Royal Coachman just after sunset.

The lake can be ice fished with reasonable success, and there is an electric motor only restriction at the lake.

Facilities

Pinantan Lake is surrounded by private homes and has two resorts with camping. Ark Park (250-573-3878 or arkpark@sympatico.ca) offers camping (with hook-ups), a general store, beaches, horseback riding, guiding and fishing equipment rental. The Pinantan Lake Resort (250-573-3534 or kcumning@direct.ca) has fully equipped 2 bedroom waterfront cottages. Boat rentals, a sandy beach and horseback riding are some of the added feature.

A public picnic area is found at the north end of the lake.

Other Options

Nearby **Paul** and **Louis Lake** are worth a try if the fish are not biting at Pinantan Lake. Also, **Little Pinantan Lake** is located at the northeast end of the main lake and is a good producer of rainbow to 1 kg (2 lbs).

Lake Definition (Pinantan Lk)

Elevation: 876 m (2,873 ft)
Surface Area: 68 ha (168 ac)
Mean Depth: 10.5 m (34.8 ft)
Max Depth: 18.5 m (60.7 ft)
Perimeter: 4,900 m (16,072 ft)
Way Point: 50° 43' 00" Lat - N
120° 02' 00" Lon - W

Recent Fish Stocking

Year	Fish Species	Life Stage	Number
1999	rainbow trout	YE	8,000
1998	rainbow trout	YE	8,000
1997	rainbow trout	YE	8,000

Pothole Lake

Access/Parking

Pothole Lake is found north of the Okanagan Connector and Kentucky-Alleyne Recreation Area. The lake is reached by travelling to the Loon Lake Exit on the Okanagan Connector. Follow the Loon Lake Road as it parallels the Okanagan Connector in a northwest direction. At a little more than 2 km northwest of the interchange, a logging road heads north. Follow that road and take a left at all the major intersections. You will reach the lake after some exploring. The Backroad Mapbook for the Kamloops/Okanagan will help you locate this and many other lakes in the area.

Fishing

Pothole Lake does not receives the same heavy fishing pressure as the Kentucky-Alleyne Recreation Area lakes. Therefore, it represents a more solitary alternative. The fishing begins after ice off in late April to early May and continues until ice-on in November. In the summer fishing success slows.

The fish grow rapidly so a 1.5 kg (2-4 lbs) rainbow is not uncommon. This is because of the abundance of nutrients in the lake supports good insect growth.

The lake is deep enough that trolling is effective. Most fishermen drag a gang troll (Ford Fender or Willow Leaf with worm) or small lure/spinner (Panther Martin, Flatfish or Deadly Dick) behind their boat.

The lake has some shoals and drop-offs allowing for some decent casting locations. The usual hatches of the region are found here so try to match the hatch.

Facilities

The lake has some undeveloped camping.

Other Options

South of Pothole Lake, the productive waters of **Crater, Alleyne, Kentucky, Loon** and **Bluey Lakes** are worth sampling. These lakes are highlighted earlier in the book.

Lake Definition

Elevation:	1,479 m (4,850 ft)
Surface Area:	4.3 ha (10.5 ac)
Mean Depth:	3.75 m (12.3 ft)
Max Depth:	10.7 m (35 ft)
Perimeter:	797 m (7,610 ft)
Way Point:	49° 57' 00" Lat - N
	120° 33' 00" Lon - W

Map Courtesy of Backroad Mapbook Volume III Kamloops/Okanagan

Thompson Nicola Region

Pressy Lake

Access/Parking

Pressy Lake is little more than a long, narrow expansion of the Rayfield River. It is found in the rolling hillsides typical of the south Cariboo region. The lake is tree lined except at the northeast corner of the lake where there is a nice open meadow and wetland extending out into the lake.

The lake is best accessed by heading north from Clinton to 70 Mile House on Highway #97. Take the North Bonaparte Road northeast from 70 Mile House. Pressy Lake is located right next to the good logging road after you pass Tin Cup and Komori Lakes.

Fishing

Pressy Lake provides a good fishery for rainbow trout to 1 kg (2 lbs) in size with the average fish being under a pound. The lake unfreezes in early May and after the turn over, fishing really starts to pick up. The lake is 31 m (120 ft) deep so it can easily be trolled. There are also some nice shoals particularly at the northwest corner ideal for fly casting.

Many fishermen troll a gang troll (Willow Leaf and worm), Flatfish, or other small spinner or lure. Fly fishermen who can match the hatch often connect with some nice trout. The hatches common to the region are present here.

Since the lake is deep and at 1025 m (3365 ft) in elevation, the summer slowdown is not a great concern as the waters stay fairly cool. Focus on the deeper parts of the lake in the summer time. In late September, the fishing picks up and can be very good as the fish actively feed in preparation for the winter months.

It is possible to cast from shore but a boat with a small motor (no motors over 10 hp) or a float tube is a definite advantage.

Facilities

Pressy Lake Rec Site is a small campsite located on the northeast end of the lake.

Other Options

Found along the North Bonaparte Road, Green, Tin Cup and Komori Lakes all offer a unique fishing experience:

The beautiful Green Lake is a popular recreational lake, which offers fair fishing for kokanee and rainbow (to 3 kg/ 8 lbs). Trolling is your best bet.

Tin Cup and Komori Lakes are smaller lakes that offer rainbow by fly, spin casting and trolling. Similar to most lakes in the area, these lakes suffer from winter-kill and the summer doldrums.

Lake Definition

Elevation:	1,022 m (3,352 ft)
Surface Area:	57 ha (141 ac)
Mean Depth:	7.2 m (24 ft)
Max Depth:	31 m (120 ft)
Perimeter:	10,800 m (35,424 ft)
Way Point:	51° 22' 00" Lat - N
	121° 02' 00" Lon - W

Thompson Nicola Region

Little Fort
Clinton
Cache Creek
Gold Bridge
Lillooet
Kamloops
Sicamous
Salmon Arm
Merritt
Boston Bar
Spuzzum
Pressy Lake

YOUNG LAKE FSR
BOULE
Bandello Lake
Home Lake
River
Rd
BONAPARTE
NORTH
Pressy Lake
To 70 Mile House
Rayfield
3700 Rd

Map Courtesy of Backroad Mapbook Volume III Kamloops/Okanagan

Pressy Lake Recreation Site

ROAD
Rayfield R.
BONAPARTE
NORTH
Rayfield R

N

Scale
200m 0 200m 400m 600m

Red Lake

Access/Parking

Red Lake is set below the distinctive Carbine Hill north of Kamloops Lake. Head west from Savona and cross the South Thompson River bridge. Take the second right off the Trans Canada Highway, which is the Deadman-Vidette Road leading north. Just before the Criss Creek bridge, take the Johnson Road to the right. That road crosses Criss Creek and then turns into the Criss Creek Forest Service Road. Stay on the main road to Sparks Lake. The road loops past several small ponds before it joins with the Cooper Creek Road. Take the Cooper Creek Road southbound and Red Lake will appear on the west side of the road.

The access to the lake is good, so you can get away with a 2wd truck.

Facilities

The lake has a cartop boat launch together with a rustic undeveloped camping area.

Lake Definition

Elevation: 947 m (3,107 ft)
Surface Area: 109 ha (269 ac)
Mean Depth: 5.7 m (18.7 ft)
Max Depth: 10.4 m (34 ft)
Perimeter: 9,052.6 m (29,700 ft)
50° 53' 00" Lat - N
120° 47' 00" Lon - W

Recent Fish Stocking

Year	Fish Species	Life Stage	Number
1997	rainbow trout, EB	FG	30,000
1996	EB	FG	40,000
1995	EB	FG	40,000

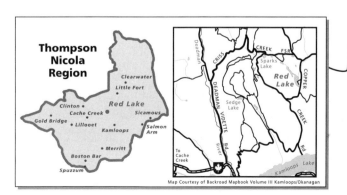

Thompson Nicola Region

Map Courtesy of Backroad Mapbook Volume III Kamloops/Okanagan

Fishing

Red Lake has a fairly good population of brook trout (to 1 kg/2 lbs) which are best fished during the fall or during ice fishing season. 60,000 brook trout were stocked in 1977 and since then, the lake has sustained a good fishery without annual stocking. Winterkill can knock back the fishery.

Spincasting and trolling small lures such as a Deadly Dick and worm is the most effective manner to fish the brook trout. Flies simply are not well received by the brook trout except in the fall when the fish congregate in the shallows for spawning. At that time, casting a large attractor type fly pattern near the weeds and shallows can produce very well.

Fly fishermen wishing to fish the lake in the spring should try a shrimp pattern. Use a sinking line and drop the fly near the bottom. Spincasting and trolling are effective in the spring and to a limited degree in the summer. That is because the waters warm significantly in the summer and the fishing slows down.

Late September- October is definitely the best time to fish. However, ice fishing using bait (worm, corn or maggot) and a hook is rewarding.

There is an engine power restriction (less than 10hp) at the lake.

Other Options

Around the Red Lake area is a series of tiny mountain lakes (**Sparks Lake**, **Moutray Lake**, **Cayuse Lake** and **Wadley Lake**). Each of these lakes can offer decent fly fishing and spincasting for trout.

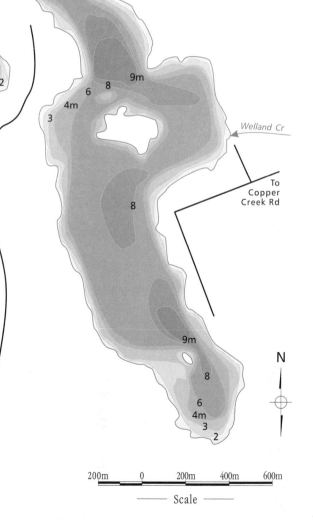

Reflector Lake

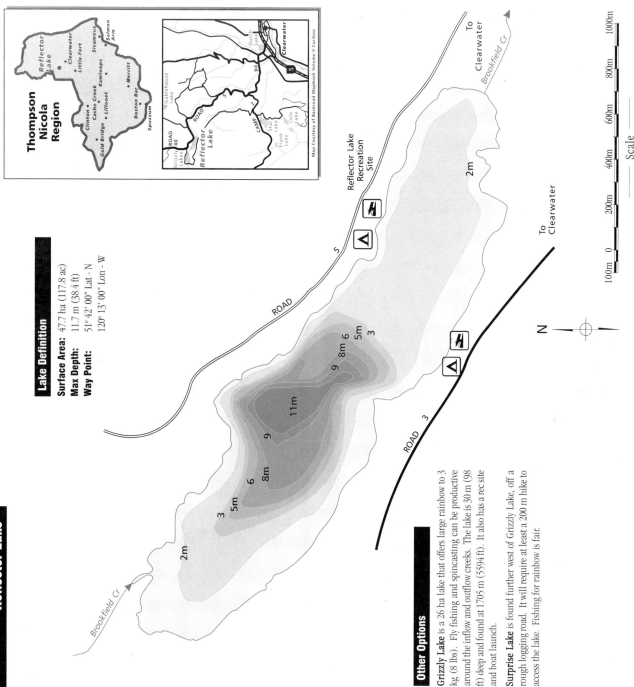

Thompson Nicola Region

Lake Definition

Surface Area: 47.7 ha (117.8 ac)
Max Depth: 11.7 m (38.4 ft)
Way Point: 51° 42' 00" Lat - N
120° 13' 00" Lon - W

Access/Parking

Reflector Lake is located northwest of Clearwater. Take the Camp 2 Road heading west from the town of Clearwater and at the second major junction, take Road 5 heading north. That road leads to the north end of Reflector Lake. To reach the south end of Reflector Lake, take the third major road (Rd 3) heading north.

Fishing

The southeast and northwest ends of Reflector Lake are extremely shallow (2-3 m/5-10 ft deep) so they are great areas for insect and aquatic invertebrate growth. The lake is only 11 m (35 ft) deep in the center. The water drops off quickly from the shallows of the southeast and northwest ends into this deep pole.

Reflector Lake holds fair numbers of rainbow to 2 kg (4-5 lbs) with the average fish being in the 30-40 cm (12-16") range. Check with the locals before heading out in the spring to see whether winterkill severely effected the fish stock.

The lake is open for fishing by the early part of May after the ice leaves and turn over occurs. Fly fishing or spincasting the fringe areas between the deep hole and the shallows are your best bet. For fly fishermen, the hatches common to the region are present. Take some time and see what the hatch is and then try to imitate it. Trolling a gang troll, Flatfish, attractor type fly (Leech, muddler minnow or Doc Spratley) or small lure can also produce. Troll around the center of the lake near the drop-offs and keep your gear near the surface to avoid weed hang-ups.

Given the shallow nature of the lake, fishing falls off in early July and does not pick up until late September. October is a good time to visit the lake as the fish are actively feeding in preparation for the ice over in mid-November.

Facilities

There are two rec sites on the shores of this lake. Reflector Lake South Recreation Site is at the southeast end of the lake and is undeveloped. Reflector Lake North Recreation Site is found off Road 2 and has a cartop boat launch, 2 camping spots and a picnic table.

Other Options

Grizzly Lake is a 26 ha lake that offers large rainbow to 3 kg (8 lbs). Fly fishing and spincasting can be productive around the inflow and outflow creeks. The lake is 30 m (98 ft) deep and found at 1705 m (5594 ft). It also has a rec site and boat launch.

Surprise Lake is found further west of Grizzly Lake, off a rough logging road. It will require at least a 200 m hike to access the lake. Fishing for rainbow is fair.

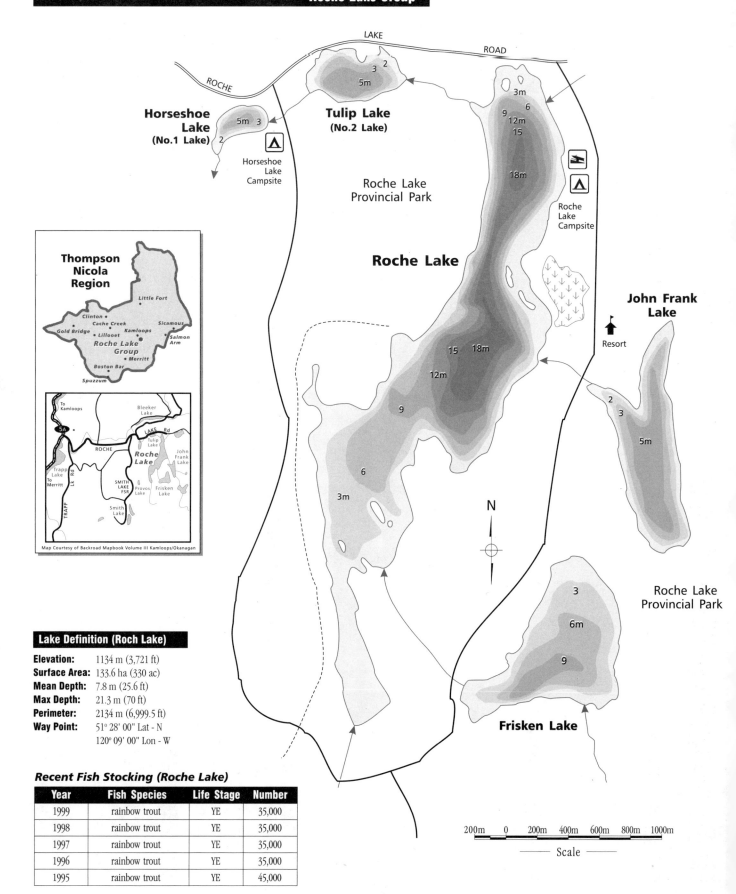

LAKE ROAD

ROCHE

Horseshoe Lake
(No.1 Lake)

5m 3

2

Horseshoe Lake Campsite

Tulip Lake
(No.2 Lake)

3 2

5m

3m

6

9

12m

15

18m

Roche Lake Campsite

Roche Lake Provincial Park

Roche Lake

15 18m

12m

9

6

3m

John Frank Lake

Resort

2

3

5m

Roche Lake Provincial Park

N

3

6m

9

Frisken Lake

Thompson Nicola Region

Little Fort

Clinton • Cache Creek • Sicamous

Gold Bridge • Kamloops

Lillooet • Salmon Arm

Roche Lake Group

Merritt

Boston Bar

Spuzzum

To Kamloops

Bleeker Lake

5A

LAKE Rd

ROCHE

Tulip Lake

Roche Lake

John Frank Lake

Trapp Lake

To Merritt

TRAPP Lk Rd

SMITH LAKE FSR

Provos Lake

Frisken Lake

Smith Lake

Map Courtesy of Backroad Mapbook Volume III Kamloops/Okanagan

Lake Definition (Roch Lake)

Elevation: 1134 m (3,721 ft)
Surface Area: 133.6 ha (330 ac)
Mean Depth: 7.8 m (25.6 ft)
Max Depth: 21.3 m (70 ft)
Perimeter: 2134 m (6,999.5 ft)
Way Point: 51° 28' 00" Lat - N
120° 09' 00" Lon - W

Recent Fish Stocking (Roche Lake)

Year	Fish Species	Life Stage	Number
1999	rainbow trout	YE	35,000
1998	rainbow trout	YE	35,000
1997	rainbow trout	YE	35,000
1996	rainbow trout	YE	35,000
1995	rainbow trout	YE	45,000

200m 0 200m 400m 600m 800m 1000m

— Scale —

Access/Parking (Roche Lake)

Roche Lake is considered one of the premier fishing lakes in the entire region. Novices can fish the lake but it is better suited to the expert fly fisherman as the fish are tough to catch.

At Merritt, take Exit #290 so you are driving on Highway #5A North. Take the Roche Lake Road, which is found just north of Trapp Lake on Highway #5A. The lake is 11km away from the highway on a good gravel road that can be driven by a car.

From Kamloops, simply head south on Highway #5A and before you reach Trapp Lake, the Roche Lake Road will head off to the east. Follow the Roche Lake Road for 11km to Roche Lake.

From Roche Lake, the access road heads south along the eastside of Roche Lake next to the powerline. John Frank Lake is the first lake south of Roche Lake and Frisken Lake is the second lake. The access road is rough and if you are visiting the lakes in the early spring or after a good rain, bring a 4wd vehicle as some of the mud holes swallow trucks.

Fishing (Roche Lake)

Fishing at Roche Lake begins to heat up in early May shortly after ice-off and runs until late October. The lake is highly productive and full of suspended nutrients ideal for insect proliferation. Thus, there is an abundant population of chironomids, sedges, damselflies, mayflies, dragonflies, leeches, water boatmen and freshwater shrimp (scuds). The food source ensures plenty of rainbow in the 1.5-2 kg (3-5 lbs) range but they are cagey.

The lake has some huge shoals and expansive weed beds. There are also several islands around the lake and many bays to explore. Needless to say, this is an ideal situation for a fly fisherman. The clear waters mean the fish are spooked easily.

Most fishermen troll the lake for the rainbow using a Wedding Ring, leech pattern or Flat Fish. Because the fishing pressure is intense, trollers end up catching most of the stocked rainbow before they reach their second year. The fly fishermen has a better chance of catching veterans by casting a line near the drop-offs or near one of the many shoals that line the lake. Practicing catch and release will help ensure a good fishery in the future.

Roche Lake has a good chironomid hatch, which occurs each spring. Sinking a chironomid pattern to the depths of the lake and then retrieving it slowly is very effective. The problem is, matching the hatch is quite difficult as there are so many variations of chironomids in the lake. Start with a #12-16 black, olive green or brown pattern and if those don't work, start exploring.

There is a declining but still very productive damselfly hatch beginning in late May- early June. A pale green imitation is the fly of choice.

The lake also has some good hatches of caddisflies, mayflies, and dragonflies. The caddisfly hatch is particularly worth fishing. Shrimp patterns can be successful in June and again in October.

In July and August, the summer doldrums hit with a vengeance. Troll or fly fish deep and slow using a nymph pattern or leech. Trolling a Willow Leaf and worm deep still works.

It is not until late September to early October where the fishing picks up again. This is a good late season lake.

Please note that there is no ice fishing allowed, you can only use a single hook and there is a daily limit of 2 rainbow. Also, a boat or float tube is a virtual necessity.

Fishing (Frisken & John Frank Lk)

Frisken Lake is very shallow as it has a maximum depth of 9 m (30 ft) near the south end. As a result, the lake is very susceptible to winterkill. If you intend to fish the lake in early spring, it is well advised that you talk to the regional biologist or some locals to see if the fish survived the previous winter.

The lake is highly productive and if the fish enter their second year, they reach the 2 kg (5 lb) range. The lake is stocked annually and those fish are known to reach 1 kg (2 lbs) by the late fall.

Beginning in mid to late May, the chironomid hatch is in full swing. Try a dark coloured chironomid pupa such as brown, black or dark green. A late June sedge hatch is worth mentioning.

The lake also has good hatches of caddisflies, damselflies, mayflies and dragonflies running through to the end of June and early July. The insect and fish activity drops off mid-July and August as the summer slowdown hit. The fishing and hatches pick up into late September and continue right through to the end of October.

The lake has an ice fishing ban, a single barbless hook restriction, a bait ban and a daily limit of two rainbow.

John Frank Lake is a shallow lake (maximum 4.5 m/15 ft) which is subject to summer drawdown as there is an irrigation dam on the lake. The lake has a real problem with winterkill but like Frisken Lake, the stocked rainbow grow rapidly in the nutrient rich lake. As a result, the rainbow approach 1 kg (2 lbs) by the fall and if they survive the winter, the fish can reach 2 kg (5 lbs).

The shallows of this dark, tea-coloured lake are overgrown with lily pads. Try casting a leech, damselfly nymph or dragonfly nymph pattern near the lily pads as the fish cruise the shallow zone in search of insects.

The lake has an ice fishing ban, a single barbless hook restriction and a bait ban.

Other Options

Horseshoe and **Tulip Lakes** are part of Roche Lake Provincial Park.

Tulip Lake is found off the Roche Lake Road before you reach Roche Lake. Horseshoe Lake is found on the second spur road heading south after you enter the Roche Lake Provincial Park. Make sure you don't take the Smith Lake Forest Service Road.

Horseshoe Lake has both brook trout and rainbow to 3 kg with the average fish being much smaller because of a winterkill problem. The 12 ha lake, which is at 1115 m (3660 ft) in elevation, is best fish using bait or by spincasting in the spring or fall or by ice fishing in the winter. Fly fishing using a shrimp, dragonfly or damselfly pattern can be productive at times.

Tulip Lake is a long narrow lake, which holds a good population of stocked brook trout growing to 1 kg (2 lbs). The fish are best fished in the fall before spawning season and in the winter. The lake is at 1115 meters in elevation and is 8 ha in size.

For the brook trout in both Tulip and Horseshoe Lake, spincasting and trolling small lures such as a Deadly Dick and worm is the most effective manner to fish them. Flies simply are not well received by the brook trout except in the fall when the fish congregate in the shallows for spawning. At that time, casting a large attractor type fly pattern near the weeds and shallows can produce very well.

An aerator was installed at Horseshoe Lake and Tulip Lake to counteract winterkill. The aerators make the ice very thin in the winter.

There is undeveloped camping and a cartop boat launch on Tulip Lake. The old Horseshoe Lake Rec Site is found at the south end of that lake and has a rustic campground together with a cartop boat launch.

Facilities

Roche Lake Provincial Park encompasses a series of 9 nutrient rich, highly productive fishing lakes. Within the provincial park is the Roche Lake Resort as well as a series of rec sites with a total of 75 camping spots.

The Roche Lake Resort (250-828-2007) is a full service resort with a main lodge located next to the lake as well as a series of attractive, cedar chalets set back from the lake. The chalets are fully furnished with a vaulted ceiling, kitchenette, fireplace and full bathrooms. The resort also offers a swimming pool, fly fishing lessons, boat rentals, mini store, guide services, jacuzzi and dock.

There is a cartop boat launch and camping at Frisken Lake. No developed facilities are located at John Frank Lake.

Salmon Lake

Access/Parking

Salmon Lake is part of the Douglas Lake but unlike other lakes in the ranch, this lake is open to the public for use. There is a charge to launch your boat, however.

Salmon Lake is easily accessed on the Douglas Lake Road. To reach the road, simply drive on Highway #5A to the beginning of the Douglas Lake Road near the north end of Nicola Lake. The Douglas Lake Road is a good, all weather access road.

From the north, head west of Falkland on Highway #97 and after passing through the tiny community of Westwold, you will see the Douglas Lake Road heading south.

Fishing

Salmon Lake is a popular fly fishing destination, which holds good numbers of rainbow that average 1 kg (2-3 lbs). Since the lake is an artificial fly only lake, trolling or casting a fly are the two methods of fishing.

Most fly fishermen cast towards the weed beds that line the west side of the lake using a damselfly (green), shrimp or chironomid pattern. In fall, backswimmer, bead-head leech and Doc Spratley patterns work well. Trolling a leech pattern is also effective. The lake is quite shallow and awfully silty so it warms significantly in the summer prompting an algae bloom and poor fishing. If that doesn't discourage you from fishing in the summer months, try a dry fly or try trolling a slow sinking line. Either way, the fly will remain near the surface and the algae will not affect your presentation as much.

There is no ice fishing, a bait ban and you must use a single barbless hook.

Facilities

The Salmon Lake Resort is part of the Douglas Lake Ranch (1-800-663-4838 or resort@douglaslake.com) and has one and two-bedroom cottages with full kitchens, electric heat and wood-burning stoves. A convenience store, outdoor heated pool and boat launch help you enjoy the resort. There are also RV and tenting sites at the resort.

Other Options

The Douglas Lake Road gives good access to a few other large lakes including **Douglas Lake** and **Chapperon Lake**. These lakes are described on page 16.

For a smaller lake experience, **Sawmill (Burnell) Lake** is found to the northwest along the Jimmy Lake Road. This stocked lake can be trolled or try fly fishing or spin casting in the spring and fall. The rainbow can reach 1 kg (2 lbs).

Lake Definition

Elevation:	1,183.5 m (3,883 ft)
Surface Area:	149.3 ha (368.9 ac)
Mean Depth:	6.7 m (22.1 ft)
Max Depth:	17.7 m (58 ft)
Perimeter:	10,076.8 m (33,960 ft)
Way Point:	51° 14' 00" Lat - N
	120° 21' 00" Lon - W

Recent Fish Stocking

Year	Fish Species	Life Stage	Number
1998	rainbow trout	FF	5,000
1995	rainbow trout	FF	6,000

Thompson Nicola Region

Map Courtesy of Backroad Mapbook Volume III Kamloops/Okanagan

Access/Parking

Saskum Lake is found near the Barriere Lakes. Head north on Highway #5 from Kamloops to Barriére where you will find the Barriére Lakes Road. This paved road heads east up the Barriére River Valley. After 17.5 km you will come to a three-way intersection, take a left heading north along the North Barriére Lake Forest Service Road. The road will soon lead along the northern shores of North Barriére Lake. After leaving that lake, cross the Barriére River bridge and take the next major road heading north. The mainhaul logging road, called the Saskum Lake Forest Service Road, will take you to the south end of the lake.

Fishing

Saskum Lake has a combination of rainbow trout, dollies and kokanee. The rainbows and dollies can reach 2 kg (4-5 lbs) in size and tend to average 0.75 kg (1-2 lbs). The kokanee are up to 1 kg (2 lbs) but are usually quite small.

Fishing is generally slow from ice-off in early May to when the lake freezes over in November. The preferred method of fishing is trolling. For the dollies, try a plug or spoon such as an Apex, Krokodile or large Flatfish. Earlier in the spring and late in the fall, you can fish near the surface in 3-6 m (10-20 ft) of water but as the summer approaches, the fish move into the depths so try at the 10-25 m (30-90 ft) level.

Both the rainbow and the kokanee take a Willow Leaf and worm. Rainbows also strike small lures such as a Wedding Ring, Flatfish or Mepps. Try trolling an attractor type fly for the rainbow like a leech or Doc Spratley.

Fly fishermen will be a little disappointed with this lake. They should focus their efforts at the outflow and inflow to the Barriére River located at the south and north ends of the lake.

Facilities

Saskum Lake has a rec site at the south end with a boat launch and sandy beach. There are 25 camping units in the rec site so you are likely to find a camping spot even on a long weekend.

Other Options

Saskum Lake is found in the Barriére Lakes region. You can find detailed descriptions of East, North and South Barriére Lakes throughout this book.

Lake Definition

Elevation:	853 m (2,798 ft)
Surface Area:	115 ha (284 ac)
Mean Depth:	18 m (59 ft)
Max Depth:	33.7 m (111 ft)
Perimeter:	5,340 m (17,515 ft)
Way Point:	51° 24' 00" Lat - N
	119° 42' 00" Lon - W

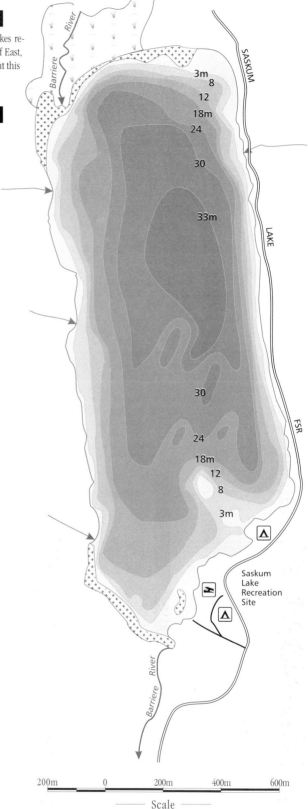

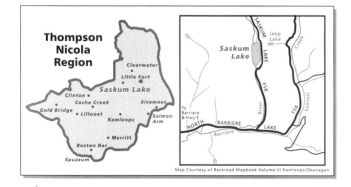

Scot Lake

Access/Parking

Scot Lake is located southwest of Bonaparte Lake. To access the lake, your best bet is to follow the North Bonaparte Road from either Highway 24 or 97. Continue to the Rayfield River and look for the Egan-Bonaparte Forest Service Road (3200 Rd). Follow that road south, past Moose Lake and Little Scot Lake all the way to a short spur road leading to the north end of Scot Lake.

If you reach Hammer Lake on the Egan-Bonaparte Forest Service Road you have gone too far. It is well advised to bring a copy of the Backroad Mapbook for the Kamloops/ Okanagan to help you find Scot Lake.

Facilities

The long drive and rough access deters vehicles with trailers. **Scot Lake Rec Site** provides 7 camping spots, including 4 picnic tables, and a boat launch at the north end of the lake. The reedy shoreline and lack of scenery makes this a better fishing lake than camping area.

Other Options

The Bonaparte Plateau offers litterally hundreds of lakes to sample. Near by **Little Scot Lake**, **Hammer Lake** and **Lastcourse Lake** offer good spring and fall rainbow fishing.

Fishing

Scot Lake is a small lake with a reedy shoreline. Good fishing is possible for rainbow in the 1 kg (1-2 lbs) range. Expansive shoals are located at the inflow creek at the southwest end of the lake and at the outflow area at the northeast end of the lake. The lake has a maximum depth of 17 m (55 ft) with two distinct potholes, one towards the northeast end of the lake and one near the middle of the lake.

After ice-off in early May, the lake is best trolled for the rainbow using a gang troll, Flatfish or small lure. Trolling around the drop-off is ideal.

Fly Fishermen should focus their efforts around the shoals at the southwest and northeast ends of the lake. The usual hatches for the region are common at this lake. Try to match one of the hatches.

By summer, the fishing slows down with the best time to fish in the early morning or in the late evening. Trolling deep in one of the two potholes or use a sinking line and fly fishing a shrimp or nymph pattern into the depths are your best chance. By late fall, good insect hatches start occurring again and fishing picks up.

Lake Definition

Elevation: 1,185 m (3,887 ft)
Surface Area: 29 ha (72 ac)
Mean Depth: 5.7 m (18.7 ft)
Max Depth: 17 m (55.8 ft)
Perimeter: 3,685 m (12,087 ft)
Way Point: 51° 15' 00" Lat - N
120° 45' 00" Lon - W

Thompson Nicola Region

Scot Lake Recreation Site

To Hammer Lake

FSR

EGAN-BONAPARTE

Scale

100m   0   100m   200m

Scuitto Lake

Access/Parking

Scuitto Lake is located southwest of the tiny community of Bestwick in the heart of rangeland. The lake is best reached by taking the Barnhartvale Road from the Trans Canada Highway east of Kamloops. Continue past the community of Barnhartvale to the Robins-Campbell Range Road and that main logging road will take you south to Bestwick. Take the road heading southwest from Bestwick along the northern shores of Campbell Lake and you will soon reach Scuitto Lake.

It is possible to reach Scuitto Lake from the south by taking the Roche Lake Road from Highway #5A. When you reach the Roche Lake Provincial Park, take a right at the Bleeker Lake Road and hang on as you pound your way north on a rough road leading past Bleeker Lake and Hosli Lake before finally reaching Scuitto Lake.

Access to Scuitto Lake is through private property, be sure to get permission before fishing the lake.

Fishing

Scuitto Lake provides good fly fishing for rainbow that average under 2 kg (4-5 lbs) in size but can reach 5 kg. The shallow, 50 ha lake has dark, nutrient-rich water, which warms in the summer resulting in an algae bloom and poor fishing.

The lake is only 8 m (27 ft) deep and has a large island in the middle, which is surrounded by inviting shoals. The area north of the island is the deepest part of the lake.

Given the depth, the lake is tough to troll unless you are fishing for "weed trout". Trolling a fly or small lure near the surface in the spring or late fall can be productive. For fly fishermen, the late spring sedge hatch is the best time to fly fish.

Please be careful as wind can play havoc on boaters. There is a daily limit of two rainbow at the lake.

Facilities

There are no developed facilities at the lake.

Other Options

Nearby **Campbell** and **Hosli Lakes** are described on page 14 in this book.

Lake Definition

Elevation:	1,041.2 m (3,416 ft)
Surface Area:	93.8 ha (231.7 ac)
Max Depth:	8.2 m (27 ft)
Way Point:	50° 33' 00" Lat - N
	120° 08' 00" Lon - W

To Campbell Lake

To Kamloops

BLEEKER LAKE

FSR

To Roche Lake & hwy 5A

20m
15
10m
5
25
10m
5
15
5
10m
5
15m
20m
10m
15
5
10m

N

Scale
100m 0 100m 200m 300m 400m 500m

Thompson Nicola Region

Little Fort
Sicamous
Salmon Arm
Clinton
Cache Creek
Kamloops
Gold Bridge
Lillooet
Merritt
Boston Bar
Spuzzum
Scuitto Lake

Curry Lake
To Kamloops
Bestwick
Campbell Lake
White Lake
CAMPBELL RANGE Rd
SCUITTO CREEK FSR
Scuitto Lake
BLEEKER LAKE FSR
Talmage Lake
Hosli Lake
To Hwy 5A

Map Courtesy of Backroad Mapbooks Volume III Kamloops/Okanagan

Skookum Lake

Access/Parking

Skookum Lake is found in the heart of the Deadman Valley. This dramatic dry valley does not see the crowds common to other areas of the region.

To reach the lake, take the Deadman-Vidette Road leading north from the Trans Canada Highway just west of the Deadman River Bridge. The road follows the Deadman River for what appears like an eternity until you reach Skookum Lake.

It is also possible to reach the lake from Highway #97 by taking the Clinton-Loon Lake Road to Vidette. Head south past Vidette Lake and you will soon reach Deadman Lake and eventually Skookum Lake on the Deadman-Vidette Road. Beyond, Deadman Lake, it is well advised that you have a 4wd vehicle, as the road is extremely rough.

Fishing

Skookum Lake is a shallow (maximum 9 m/30 ft) lake with some nice shoals at the southeast end and at the north end. The lake drops off rapidly particularly at the east and west ends of the lake.

Fishing is best beginning in mid-May after the lake has turned over and before mid-July. By the summer, the fish are very inactive as the water has warmed because of the shallow depths. It is not until late September that the fishing picks up again.

Skookum Lake contains both rainbow and kokanee that can reach 1 kg (2 lbs) in size. Trolling is tough because of the shallow depths but it is possible to troll a gang troll, fly or small lure near the surface. For the kokanee, try a Willow Leaf and worm or maggot. A pink lure such as a Dick Nite or pink Flatfish also works for the kokanee. The rainbow like a Willow Leaf and worm as well as small lures.

Fly fishermen should focus their efforts around the shoals and the nice drop-offs. Most of the insect hatches common to the region are also found at this lake. Try matching one of the many hatches.

Facilities

Skookum Lake Rec Site has 15 camping spots in a large grassy area next to the lake. There is a cartop boat launch at the site.

Other Options

Skookum Lake is part of a series of good fishing lakes along the Deadman-Vidette Road. **Mowich, Snohoosh, Deadman** and **Vidette Lakes** are all highlighted throughout this book.

Lake Definition

Elevation:	807.9 m (2,650 ft)
Surface Area:	18.8 ha (46.5 ft)
Mean Depth:	4.5 m (14.8 ft)
Max Depth:	8.8 m (29 ft)
Perimeter:	2,222 m (7,290 ft)
Way Point:	51° 07' 00" Lat - N
	120° 53' 00" Lon - W

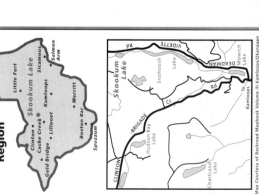

Map Courtesy of Backroad Mapbook Volume III Kamloops/Okanagan

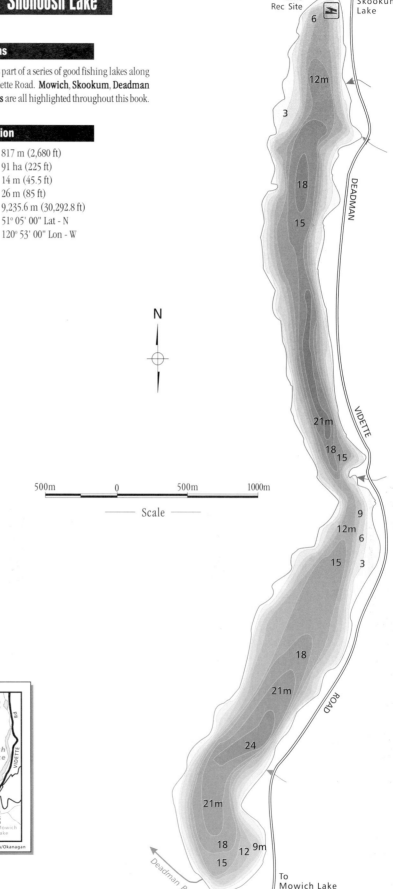

Snohoosh Lake

Access/Parking

At the east end of Kamloops Lake, the Trans Canada Highway crosses the Thompson River on an impressive bridge. Head north from the bridge and you will soon cross the Deadman River. The Deadman-Vidette Road leads directly north from the west side of the Deadman River Bridge. Stay on the main logging road avoiding any detours. The first lake you will reach is Mowich Lake, which will be on the west left side of the road. A few kilometers to the north, Snohoosh Lake will also appear on the left.

Fishing

Snohoosh Lake is a long, narrow lake containing both rainbow trout and kokanee that can reach 1 kg (2 lbs) in size and are best caught by trolling.

Fishing is best beginning in mid-May after the lake has turned over and before mid-July. By the summer, the fish are very inactive as the water has warmed because of the shallow depths and low elevation. It is not until late September that the fishing picks up again.

Trolling is popular at the lake. Use a gang troll, fly or small lure. For the kokanee, try a Willow Leaf and worm or maggot. A pink lure such as a Dick Nite or pink Flatfish also works for the kokanee. The rainbow like a Willow Leaf and worm as well as small lures.

Fly fishermen should focus their efforts around the shoals and the nice drop-offs. Most of the insect hatches common to the region are also found at this lake so try matching one of the hatches.

Using a float tube or boat improve the chances of success. In the summer months, it is possible to shore fish because the water level tends to drop.

Facilities

The **Snoohoosh Lake Rec Site** is at the north end of the lake. It has a boat launch and 5 treed camping sites. Shore casting from the rec site is a possibility in the summer months when the lake is at its lowest water level. A private campground is located at the south end of the lake.

Other Options

Snohoosh Lake is part of a series of good fishing lakes along the Deadman-Vidette Road. **Mowich**, **Skookum**, **Deadman** and **Vidette Lakes** are all highlighted throughout this book.

Lake Definition

Elevation: 817 m (2,680 ft)
Surface Area: 91 ha (225 ft)
Mean Depth: 14 m (45.5 ft)
Max Depth: 26 m (85 ft)
Perimeter: 9,235.6 m (30,292.8 ft)
Way Point: 51° 05' 00" Lat - N
120° 53' 00" Lon - W

N

500m   0   500m   1000m

Scale

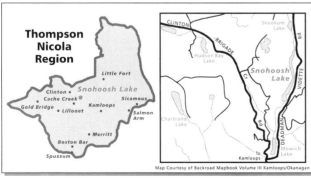

Map Courtesy of Backroad Mapbook Volume III Kamloops/Okanagan

Stake Lake

Access/Parking

State Lake is easily accessed by taking the Lac Le Jeune Exit (Exit 336) on the Coquihalla Connector between Merritt and Kamloops. Head east on the paved Lac Le Jeune Road and after passing the turn-off to Lac Le Jeune, you will see Stake Lake on the right. A car or RV can easily reach the lake.

For a more scenic route, travel south on the Lac Le Jeune Road from Kamloops.

Fishing

The Stake Lake fishing season begins in late April when the ice leaves the lake. There are fair numbers of rainbow trout that grow to 2 kg (4–5 lbs) but the average size of the fish is quite small. You should expect to see other fishermen as the lake is often crowded.

State Lake is best fished, like most lakes, in the spring and fall. However, the summer fishery does remain active. The lake has an aerator to guard against winterkill and it is stocked annually to counteract the heavy fishing pressure.

The mainstay of the lake is trolling a Willow Leaf and worm or small lure such as a Flatfish or Dick Nite. However, fly fishing should not be ruled out as the lake has some nice shoals and weed covered shallows to sample. Be forewarned, the crystal clear water makes the fly fishing tough as the fish are harder to trick and are extremely picky. Try using a long fine leader to counteract the clear water problem.

The caddisfly hatch at the end of May and into early June is a good time to dry fly fish. A shrimp pattern, fished near the bottom, is also effective throughout most of the spring and the fall. Other hatches of note are the spring chironomid hatch, the spring mayfly hatch and the fall water boatman hatch.

For best results, use a float tube and cast near the shoals and drop-offs, which are easily seen through the clear water.

Ice fishing is not recommended as the aerator makes the ice dangerously thin.

Facilities

State Lake is the focus of a popular recreation area given the network of X-C ski trails, biking and hiking trails. Although there is no camping on State Lake, there is camping in the State-McConnell Recreation Area. A nice picnic area is at the lake and there is a cartop boat launch.

Lake Definition

Elevation: 1,335 m (4,378.8 ft)
Surface Area: 25 ha (61.8 ac)
Mean Depth: 3.9 m (12.8 ft)
Max Depth: 8.7 m (28.5 ft)
Perimeter: 2,640 m (8,659 ft)
Way Point: 50° 31' 55" Lat - N
120° 29' 30" Lon - W

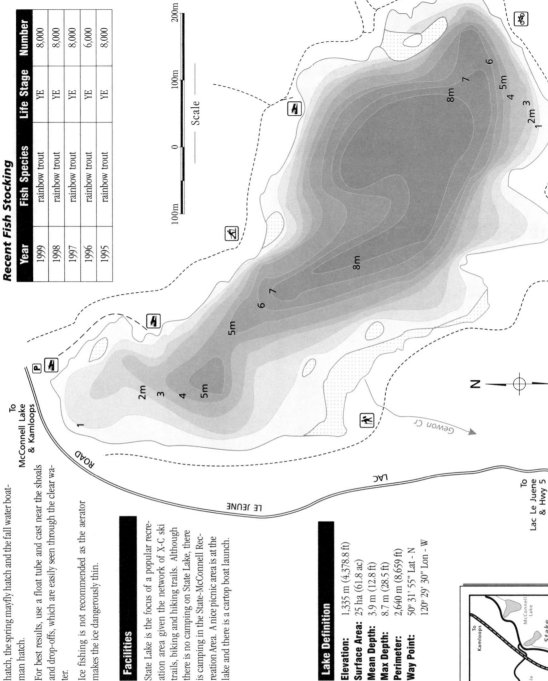

Recent Fish Stocking

Year	Fish Species	Life Stage	Number
1999	rainbow trout	YE	8,000
1998	rainbow trout	YE	8,000
1997	rainbow trout	YE	8,000
1996	rainbow trout	YE	6,000
1995	rainbow trout	YE	8,000

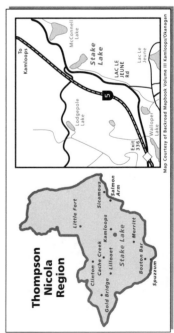

Thompson Nicola Region

Map Courtesy of Backroad Mapbook Volume III Kamloops/Okanagan

Stukemapten Lake

Map Courtesy of Backroad Mapbook Volume III Kamloops/Okanagan

Access/Parking

To reach this remote lake requires a lot of driving guaranteed to rattle your teeth and clog your lungs with dust.

From the Trans Canada Highway 5.5 km northeast of Chase, take the Squilax-Anglemont Road leading north. This paved road immediately crosses a bridge over the Shuswap Lake and then heads north. Soon you will have to turn left at the first major intersection and follow the paved Holdings Road that winds gently along the western banks of the Adams River to the south end of the lake. Continue northward along the Holdings Road to the mill and from there, an excellent, well graded but windy mainhaul logging road will bring you to the north end of the Adams Lake.

From the north end of the Adams Lake, take the Adams East Road so you are heading south along the eastern shores of the Adams Lake. The third main road leading to the right is the Momich-Stukemapten Forest Service Road. That mainhaul road leads right through the heart of the Momich Lake Provincial Park past the three lakes. Hang a left on Cayenne Main after you pass by the third lake and you will soon reach Stukemapten Lake.

Facilities

There are no developed facilities at the lake. Nearby Momich Lake Provincial Park has three designated camping areas, one on the shores of the Adams Lake and two on the shores of Momich Lake. If you want to camp closer to Stukemapten Lake, several pull outs along the logging road can be used.

Fishing

The lake is found above the Momich River Valley and so the ice leaves the lake a little later than the Momich Lakes (early May). Once the ice is off, it is best to troll for the rainbow to 2 kg (5 lbs).

Despite the remote access, the lake does not offer incredible fishing. Trolling a gang troll (Wedding Wing and worm) or a small lure is your best bet. Try focussing along the prominent drop-offs on the eastern and western shores.

If you are set on fly fishing or spincasting, the shoals at the north and south end of the lake look inviting. These areas are also the location of the inflow and outflow creeks so the fish tend to congregate in the shallows in search of food.

Other Options

Momich Lakes are highlighted on page 59.

Further to the east, **Humamilt Lake** is a long narrow lake that is actually made up of a chain of three lakes. This low elevation, 465 ha lake offers good fishing for small rainbow in the spring and fall. Try fly fishing or trolling. There are rec sites and boat launches on both the western and eastern end of the lakes.

Lake Definition

Elevation: 594 m (1,948 ft)
Surface Area: 119 ha (294 ac)
Mean Depth: 14 m (46 ft)
Max Depth: 35 m (115 ft)
Perimeter: 7,030 m (23,058 ft)
Way Point: 51° 20' 00" Lat - N
119° 14' 00" Lon - W

Stump Lake

Access/Parking

Stump Lake is one of the better large rainbow producing lakes in the Thompson/Nicola region. The lake is located right next to Highway #5A northeast of Nicola Lake. Simply take the Highway #5A Exit from the Coquihalla Connector at Merritt and you will soon reach the lake after passing by Nicola Lake. Stump Lake is the first large lake located on the east side of the highway.

Alternatively, head south from Kamloops on the highway and you will soon reach the lake. Either way, the access to the lake is good allowing cars and RVs to reach the lake.

Fishing

The ice leaves the lake by late March so the fishing season starts early. Despite its easy access and productive water, the lake does not receive a lot of fishing pressure because it is noted for being extremely difficult to fish. The fish are hard to catch and the wind can play havoc on boaters. Also, in periods of drought, the lake has an alkalinity problem and the fish survival plummets.

When the lake has a good inflow of water and is being flushed, the lake becomes very fertile with a lot of insect and aquatic invertebrates. It is at that time, a good fly presentation can be very productive.

Stump Lake produces large rainbow (to 5 kg/10 lbs), brook trout (to 2 kg/4-5 lbs) and kokanee (to 1-2 kg/ 2-4 lbs). The large number of insects and zooplankton attribute to the fish size. Since the lake is at 750 m (2500 ft) in elevation and is shallow, it tends to warm during the summer so it is best to concentrate your efforts in the spring and fall.

Trolling is the mainstay of the lake although fly fishermen may wish to try their luck at the south and north end of the lakes where the shoals and weeds offer good natural habitat for the rainbow. In the spring and fall, trollers do well troll-

ing a fly near the surface or by trolling a Willow Leaf and worm. If you want to fish the lake in the summer, try trolling a nymph pattern or a leech deep and slow. Also, a Willow Leaf and worm trolled deep continues to be a good choice.

In the summer months, kokanee fishing can be fairly good if you wait until there is a chop on the water and you then troll a pink Apex, pink Flatfish or wedding band near the surface very slowly.

Fly fishermen will be most productive if you use a shrimp pattern on a sinking line dangled near the bottom. Damselfly or dragonfly nymphs cast near the reeds works well particularly in the early spring when there is a good chance to hook one of the monster trout. Doc Spratleys or tied down minnow patterns should not be ruled out. In the summer months, black Idaho nymphs, 52 Buicks, chironomid pupae and halfbacks are particularly effective.

Facilities

The lake has a public picnic area and a boat launch off of Highway #5A. A private camping facility is at the east end of the lake.

Lake Definition

Elevation:	750 m (2,460 ft)
Surface Area:	780 ha (1,928 ac)
Mean Depth:	11.6 m (38 ft)
Max Depth:	21 m (70 ft)
Perimeter:	16,084 m (52,800 ft)
Way Point:	50° 22' 00" Lat - N
	120° 22' 00" Lon - W

Recent Fish Stocking

Year	Fish Species	Life Stage	Number
1999	rainbow trout, kokanee	FR, FG, YE	207,824
1998	rainbow trout, kokanee	FR, FG, YE	244,928
1997	rainbow trout, kokanee	FR, FG, YE	441,560
1996	rainbow trout	FF, FG, YE,	104,390
1995	rainbow trout, kokanee	FG, YE	76,589

Thompson Nicola Region

Map Courtesy of Backroad Mapbook Volume III Kamloops/Okanagan

Taweel Lake

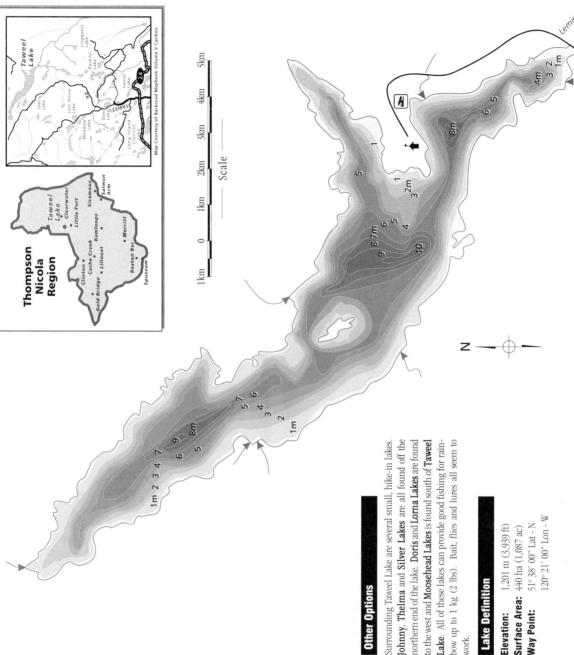

Map Courtesy of Backroad Mapbook Volume V Cariboo

Thompson Nicola Region

Taweel Lake
Clearwater
Little Fort
Sicamous
Salmon Arm
Clinton
Cache Creek
Kamloops
Merritt
Gold Bridge
Lillooet
Boston Bar
Spuzzum

Scale

1km 0 1km 2km 3km 4km 5km

N

Lemieux Cr

Access/Parking

Taweel Lake is located about 32 km northwest of Little Fort. At Little Fort, turn left on Highway #24 and continue on the highway until you reach the Taweel Lake Road. Head north on this road past a series of small pothole lakes to the southeast end of the lake. The Taweel Lake Road is a bit rough in places so a 4wd truck is a definite advantage.

Taweel Lake can also be accessed off an old road off the Lemieux Creek Road. This old road will require a 4wd vehicle to acces the lake.

Fishing

The fishing season runs from early May at ice-off to November. Perhaps due to the access, the lake does not receive the same intense fishing pressure as other lakes in the Thompson/Nicola Region.

Taweel Lake is definitely worth a try as the lake has excellent fishing for rainbow that reach 2 kg (3-4 lbs) The lake has numerous bays, rock shoals and weedbeds as well as a couple of small islands. Thus, the terrain is ideal for fish rearing.

The fishing season runs from early May at ice-off to November. The lake does not receive the same intense fishing pressure as other lakes in the Thompson/Nicola Region.

Trollers do well with the usual gang trolls or with a Flatfish. Fly fishermen should try the late June-early July caddisfly hatch. The mayfly hatch in late June-early July can also be a very good time to fly fish. Try trolling a leech pattern as well.

Spincasters can have good success casting a Deadly Dick, Flatfish, Panther Martin or Blue Fox near the drop-offs. The shoals around the small islands are a good place to focus.

Other Options

Surrounding Taweel Lake are several small, hike-in lakes. **Johnny**, **Thelma** and **Silver Lakes** are all found off the northern end of the lake. **Doris** and **Lorna Lakes** are found to the west and **Moosehead Lakes** is found south of **Taweel Lake**. All of these lakes can provide good fishing for rainbow up to 1 kg (2 lbs). Bait, flies and lures all seem to work.

Lake Definition

Elevation: 1,201 m (3,939 ft)
Surface Area: 440 ha (1,087 ac)
Way Point: 51° 38' 00" Lat - N
120° 21' 00" Lon - W

Facilities

There are two resorts (Taweel Lake Fishing Resort and the Nehalliston Fishing Camp) at the lake but no rec site or public camping.

Telfer Lake

Access/Parking

The long drive into this lake is guaranteed to limit a lot of outdoorsmen from fishing the lake. The road to the lake, however, is very good so even a car or RV could conceivably reach the lake although it is certainly not recommended.

From the Trans Canada Highway 5.5 km northeast of Chase, take the Squilax-Anglemont Road leading north. This paved road immediately crosses a bridge over the Shuswap Lake and then heads north. Soon you will have to turn left at the first major intersection and follow the paved Holdings Road that winds gently along the western banks of the Adams River to the south end of the lake. Continue northward along the Holdings Road to the mill and from there, an excellent, well graded but windy mainhaul logging road will bring you to the north end of the Adams Lake.

The Gannett Lake Forest Service Road is a major logging road heading to the left at 3.5 km on the Adams Lake East Road. This logging road is in good shape and brings you up into the Gannett Creek drainage from the Adams Lake. Telfer Lake is the first lake in the logged out drainage and requires a short hike to reach it.

Fishing

Telfer Lake offers good fishing for rainbow trout that can reach 1 kg (2.5 lbs) but average 20-25 cm (8-10"). The lake is best fly fished in the spring and fall. Spincasting from shores is possible although the use of a float tube or boat is more desirable.

The best areas of the lake to try are near the outflow creek at the southwest end of the lake or near the inflow creek at the north end of the lake. Also, try around the sunken island in the bay near the west end of the lake.

The lake is deep enough that the water does not warm significantly in the summer so the summer doldrums are not real problem.

Facilities

There are no developed facilities next to the lake. A number of roadside pull-outs and side roads can be used to camp. It is possible to launch a small boat at the lake but remember you will need to carry the boat to the lake.

Lake Definition

Elevation: 990 m (3,249 ft)
Surface Area: 48 ha (119 ac)
Mean Depth: 9 m (30 ft)
Max Depth: 21 m (69 ft)
Perimeter: 4,510 m (14,793 ft)
Way Point: 51° 27' 00" Lat - N
119° 23' 00" Lon - W

Scale
100m 0 100m 200m 300m 400m

Gannett Cr

N

FSR
LAKE
GANNETT

Gannett Cr

Thompson Nicola Region

Clearwater
Little Fort
Telfer Lake
Sicamous
Salmon Arm
Clinton
Cache Creek
Kamloops
Merritt
Gold Bridge
Lillooet
Boston Bar
Spuzzum

Gannett Lake
Telfer Lake
Gannett Creek FSR
ADAMS LAKE EAST FSR
Adams Lake
To Chase

Tranquille Lake

Access/Parking

Tranquille Lake is located south of the Porcupine Meadows Provincial Park and the Bonaparte Provincial Park in the Bonaparte Plateau region.

To reach the lake involves a long drive on a series of logging roads. From Kamloops, take the Lac Du Bois Road north. At the 15 km mark, hang a left on the Sawmill Lake Road, which takes you past Pass Lake and then Saul Lake. Northwest of Saul Lake, there is a 4 way junction with the 4020 Road. Go right on 4020 Road and that road will lead by Truda Lake and then Tranquille Lake.

Another route from Kamloops is to drive the Tranquille Road west along the shore of the Kamloops Lake. Head north on the Tranquille-Criss Cr Road (Red Lake Road), the first major road after you cross the Tranquille River. This road takes you up the Tranquille River Valley. After the road crosses the river for the last time and heads west away from the river, you will see the Tranquille River Forest Service Road heading north. Take that road to the junction with the 4200 Road. Turn east on the 4200 Road and soon you will reach the Sawmill Lake Road. Continue straight through on the 4200 Road to Tranquille Lake.

Tranquille Lake can also be reached from the Deadman River Valley by taking the Criss Creek Forest Service Road off of the Deadman- Vidette Road. The Criss Creek Forest Service Road connects with the Tranquille-Criss Creek Road north of Red Lake. Take the Tranquille-Criss Creek Road southeast to the Tranquille River Forest Service Road and follow that road to the 4200 Road and eventually the lake. If you reach the river on the Tranquille-Criss Creek Road, you have gone too far.

Fishing

Tranquille Lake, given its high 1250 m (4100 ft) elevation, is considered a good fishing lake throughout the ice-free season even in the summer. The lake has rainbow to 1 kg (2 lbs) and some small kokanee. The fish are plentiful and are more than willing to bite your line but don't expect any big ones.

Tranquille Lake is 13 m (42 ft) deep with the deepest hole being towards the northwest end of the lake. The water drops off rapidly in that area. In the rest of the lake, the water drops off gradually.

Fly fishermen use small attractor patterns like the Doc Spratley or leech patterns. Trollers, should stick to the Willow leaf and worm or maggots. Spincasters do well with a Wedding Ring, Mepps, Panther Martin or Deadly Dick.

Facilities

There is a resort at the east end of the lake offering cabins and other amenities.

Other Options

Saul Lake is found south of Tranquille Lake and is a popular lake complete with a rec site. The 25 ha lake offers small rainbow that can be taken on a fly (shrimp or attractor patterns) or by a gang troll.

Lake Definition

Elevation:	1,400 m (4,592 ft)
Surface Area:	58 ha (143 ac)
Mean Depth:	6.6 m (21.6 ft)
Max Depth:	13 m (42.6 ft)
Perimeter:	4,353 m (14,268 ft)
Way Point:	50° 56' 00" Lat - N
	120° 34' 00" Lon - W

N

Scale

100m 0 100m 200m 300m 400m 500m

To
Sawmill
Lake FSR

Rd

4020

Tranquille
River

TRANQUILLE

FSR

12m

10
8
6m
4

2m

Masters
Subalpine
Trek

Resort

Tranquille R

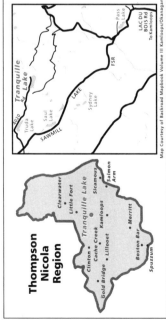

Thompson
Nicola
Region

Clearwater
Little Fort
Tranquille Lake
Salmon
Arm
Sicamous
Clinton
Cache Creek
Kamloops
Lillooet
Merritt
Gold Bridge
Boston Bar
Spuzzum

Tranquille
Lake
4020
Truda
Lake
Saul
Lake
SAWMILL
LAKE
Sydney
Lake
Pass
Lake
LAC DU
BOIS Rd
To Kamloops
FSR

Map Courtesy of Backroad Mapbook Volume III Kamloops/Okanagan

Tsikwustum Lake

Access/Parking

From the Trans Canada Highway 5.5 km northeast of Chase, take the Squilax-Anglemont Road leading north. This paved road immediately crosses a bridge over the Shuswap Lake and then heads north. Soon you will have to turn left at the first major intersection and follow the paved Holdings Road that winds gently along the western banks of the Adams River to the south end of the lake. Continue northward along the Holdings Road to the mill and from there, an excellent, well graded but windy mainhaul logging road will bring you to the north end of the Adams Lake.

From the north end of the Adams Lake, head south on the Adams East Road to the Rock Creek Main. This logging road switchbacks up the mountain side eventually leading to Tsikwustum Lake, at 1515 m (4970 ft) in elevation.

A 4wd vehicle with definitely be an advantage. Snow also affects access as the road becomes very difficult to drive by late October and is not clear until May.

Fishing

The 123 ha lake holds descent numbers of rainbow to 1 kg (2 lbs) but average 30-35 cm 12-14"). It has a later start to the fishing season given its elevation and the fact that it is not unusual to have ice on the lake in mid-May. Towards the end of May to early June, the fly fishing and spincasting can be very good as there are numerous shallows and weedbeds ideal for insect and fish rearing. Trollers are confined to the main body of the lake where the water is deepest. It is well advised to use the depth chart to avoid trolling over the shallows and hanging up your gear.

The fishing, given the lakes' elevation, remains fairly steady during the summer months. By late October, the lake begins to ice over.

Lake Definition

Elevation:	1,515 m (4,969 ft)
Surface Area:	123 ha (304 ac)
Mean Depth:	47 m (154 ft)
Max Depth:	25 m (82 ft)
Perimeter:	9,960 m (32,669 ft)
Way Point:	51° 25' 00" Lat - N
	119° 15' 00" Lon - W

Facilities

There are no developed facilities next to the lake. A number of roadside pull-outs and side roads can be used to camp. It is possible to launch a small boat at t e lake.

Other Options

Tsikwustum Lake is found in the drainage south of **Telfer** and **Gannett Lake**. Both of these lakes are highlighted earlier in this book.

Thompson Nicola Region

Clearwater
Little Fort
Sicamous
Salmon Arm
Clinton
Cache Creek
Kamloops
Tsikwustum Lake
Gold Bridge
Lillooet
Merritt
Boston Bar
Spuzzum

Gannett Lake
Telfer Lake
Tsikwustum Lake
ROCK CREEK
MAIN
EAST
FSR
ADAMS
Adams Lake

Map Courtesy of Backroad Mapbook Volume III Kamloops/Okanagan

Access/Parking

Tumtum Lake is found in the upper Adams River Valley north of Adams Lake. A very long drive brings you to the lake.

From the Trans Canada Highway 5.5 km northeast of Chase, take the Squilax-Anglemont Road leading north. This paved road immediately crosses a bridge over the Shuswap Lake and then heads north. Soon you will have to turn left at the first major intersection and follow the paved Holdings Road that winds gently along the western banks of the Adams River to the south end of the lake. Continue northward along the Holdings Road to the mill and from there, an excellent, well graded but windy mainhaul logging road will bring you to the north end of the Adams Lake.

Once at the north end of the Adams Lake, continue on the Harbour Lake Forest Service Road, which follows the Adams River and you will eventually reach the lake.

A truck is highly recommended.

Fishing

Tumtum Lake is a deep (maximum 65 m/213 ft) lake, which is best suited for trolling. The ice leaves the lake in early May and within a couple weeks, the fishing is in full swing. Try trolling along the drop-offs next to the western or eastern shores using a gang troll or small lure. You should be able to catch a few rainbow.

For fly fishermen and spincasters, the northern most bay is a good area as is the inflow and outflow to the Adams River located at the north and south ends of the lake.

Facilities

There is a small forest service rec site at the south end of the lake near the outflow to the Adams Lake. Small boats can be launched from there.

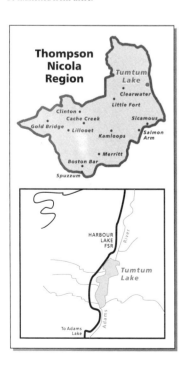

Other Options

While in this remote area, allow some time to explore some of the other lakes in the area. In particular, **Harbour Lake** is found south of Tumtum Lake. Harbour Lake is highlighted on page 33 in this book.

Lake Definition

Elevation: 652 m (2,139 ft)
Surface Area: 388 ha (959 ac)
Mean Depth: 32.1 m (105 ft)
Max Depth: 65 m (213 ft)
Perimeter: 11,400 m (37,392 ft)
Way Point: 51° 52' 00" Lat - N
119° 07' 00" Lon - W

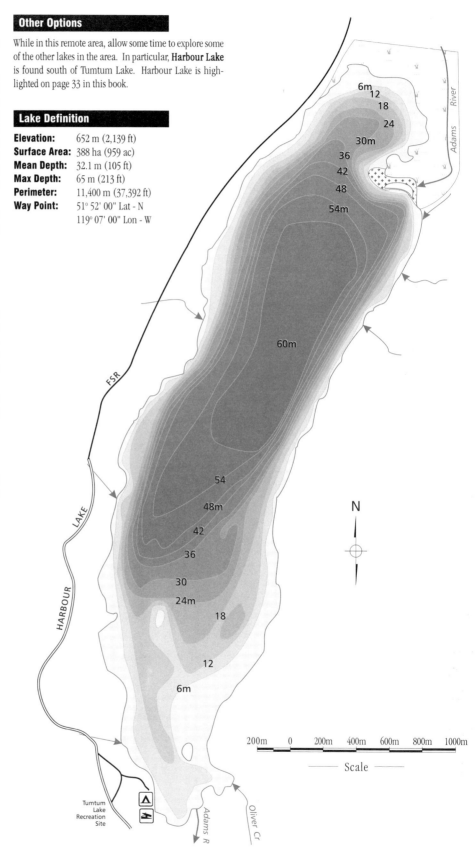

Tunkwa Lake

Access/Parking

From the Coquihalla Connector, take Exit 336 (Lac Le Jeune) south of Kamloops and head west on the Meadow Creek Road to the mining town of Logan Lake. The Tunkwa Lake Road leads north from the town and soon you will reach the Tunkwa Lake Provincial Park. The lake is on a side road off the main road and is clearly marked by signs.

Alternatively, drive a few kilometers east of Savona on the Trans Canada Highway and find the Tunkwa lake Road heading south. This road will lead into the park.

Fishing

Tunkwa Lake is a popular fishing lake with dark, murky water. In fact, it was the home of the 1993 World Fly fishing Championships. It is found in the rolling hills of the Thompson Plateau and is surrounded by an open grassy meadow dotted with lodgepole pine trees. The lake is ideal for fish rearing as it has many bowl-shaped shallows covered by weeds. Some describe the lake as one big shoal.

Fishing at Tunkwa Lake begins to heat up shortly after ice-off around May 1st and runs to the end of November. The lake is highly productive and full of suspended nutrients ideal for insect proliferation. Thus, there is an abundant population of chironomids, sedges, damselflies, mayflies, dragonflies, leeches, water boatman and freshwater shrimp.

Right after ice-off, the chironomids begin to emerge with a vengeance and continue to hatch all the way into the summer. Try a long leader with a small, dark green or black chironomid papa pattern retrieved very slowly from the depths of the lake. Also, in May, try a dark coloured nymph pattern such as a bear hair humpy or Idaho nymph with or without a crystal flasher.

As June approaches, larger, more colourful chironomid patterns are the best choice. Damselfly patterns are also a good choice as that hatch is in full swing as well. Other fly patterns that work in the spring are leech patterns trolled around the lake or shrimp, mayfly, dragonfly nymph, water boatman and bloodworm patterns cast near the weeds.

The summer months from July to early September are very poor fishing months given the algae bloom that makes casting a clean line next to impossible. Added to the algae is the inevitable drawdown of the lake for irrigation purposes.

If that doesn't discourage you from fishing in the summer then try a nymph or leech pattern fished deep. Other pat-

terns include the Tom Thumb, tri-wing sedge and humpies. Trollers should use a Willow Leaf and worm.

By late September to early October, the first frost means a decline in the algae bloom and a chance to fish again. Shrimp, chironomid and bloodworm patterns start producing along with a Tom Thumb or an elk wing caddis pattern. The fishing late in the fall can be unbelievable and some of the big fish are taken at that time of year.

Although a belly boat is helpful, it is possible to fish the lake from shore given that the shoreline is a large, open meadow.

Please note that the lake is closed to ice fishing and there is an engine restriction.

Facilities

The Tunkwa Provincial Park encompasses the lake and contains a rec site on Tunkwa and Leighton Lakes. Both rec sites have camping and a boat launch.

Tunkwa Lake Fishing Camp & Resort (250-523-9697) is located on the east side of the lake and offers rustic cabins and camping sites. The resort is open year round.

Other Options

Nearby **Leighton Lake** is a shallow lake that offers stocked rainbow that can reach 3 kg (8 lbs). Fly fishing can be good but be prepared for mixed results.

Recent Fish Stocking

Year	Fish Species	Life Stage	Number
1999	rainbow trout	YE	49,350
1998	rainbow trout	YE	49,864
1997	rainbow trout	YE	49,438

Lake Definition

Elevation:	1,144 m (3,751 ft)
Surface Area:	296 ha (731 ac)
Mean Depth:	3.7 m (12 ft)
Max Depth:	5.2 m (17 ft)
Perimeter:	12,231 m (40,128 ft)
Way Point:	50° 36' 00" Lat - N
	120° 51' 00" Lon - W

Thompson Nicola Region

Map Courtesy of Backroad Mapbook Volume III Kamloops/Okanagan

Leighton Lake

Tunkwa Cr

N

Tunkwa Provincial Park

Leighton Lake Rec Site

Tunkwa Lake Rec Site

TUNKWA LAKE FSR

6m
5
4
3m

Tunkwa Cr

500m 0   1km   2km   3km   4km   5km
——— Scale ———

Twin Lake

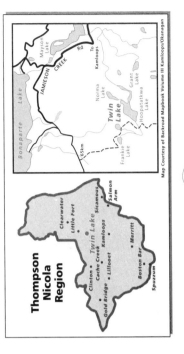

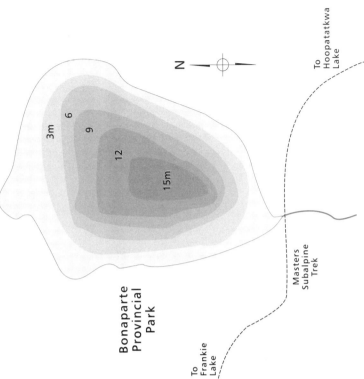

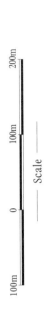

Map Courtesy of Backroad Mapbook Volume III Kamloops/Okanagan

N

To Frankie Lake

To Hoopatatkwa Lake

Bonaparte Provincial Park

Masters Subalpine Trek

Scale

Access/Parking

Twin Lake is found at the north end of Bonaparte Provincial Park. There is no road access into the lake so you will have to make a long hike from the 65 km marker on the Jamieson Creek Road or fly in to the lake.

To find the trailhead, is no easy task either. Take the Westsyde Road north of Kamloops until you reach the Jamieson Creek Road heading off to the left. The junction is on the west bank of the North Thompson River north of the Lac Du Bois Grasslands Provincial Park.

Head north on the Jamieson Creek Road avoiding the temptation to veer off the main road on one of the many logging roads leading from the Jamieson Creek Road. By the time you reach the trailhead after 65 km of gravel road you probably won't mind stretching your legs with a good walk.

Fishing

Twin Lake, due to its remote access, offers good fishing for rainbow trout to 2 kg (4-5 lbs) by fly fishing, bait fishing or spincasting.

The lake has a deep hole (16 m/50 ft) right in the middle of the lake. Also, some inviting drop-offs are located along the entire shores of the lake.

For dry fly fishermen, getting to the lake in late June or early July will reward you with a good sedge hatch. Damselfly, mayfly nymph and chironomid pupae patterns also work at varying time in the spring and fall depending on the hatch.

In the summer, the fish retreat to the deep hole. Fishing slows in the summer months but that does not rule out using a sinking line with a nymph pattern or Doc Spratley fished at the fringes to the deep hole. Also, bait fishing or spincasting into the depths of the lake at that time of year can be effective.

By the early fall, the hatches are back into full swing and fishing the drop-offs is effective again.

It is possible to fish from shore but a float tube will definitely improve success.

Facilities

The Corbett Lake Country Inn (250-378-4334) offers cedar cottages, with full kitchens and fireplaces as well as accommodation in the main lodge. Peter McVey, the owner, prides himself on fine dining with four course meals a regular event. The accommodations are reasonable ranging from $30.00 to $110.00 per night per person depending on the room, time of year and the number of people in your party. Row boats are available for rent and if you need some casting instruction or local fishing advise, Peter is certainly there to help.

A small parking lot and cartop boat launch is located at the north end of the lake away from the resort and next to the Okanagan Connector.

Other Options

Within the newly established Bonaparte Provincial Park, there is an unlimited number of small fishing lakes to explore. Many of these lakes hold rainbow, which are easily taken on a fly or by spin casting. **Frankie, Norma, Hoopatatkwa** and **Grant Lakes** are found close to **Hoopatalkwa Lake**. There are no roads into the area, which restricts access to foot or canoe.

Lake Definition

Elevation:	1,432.6 m (4,699 ft)
Surface Area:	9.77 ha (24 ac)
Mean Depth:	6.9 m (22.6 ft)
Max Depth:	16.76 m (54.97 ft)
Perimeter:	1,257 m (4,124 ft)
Way Point:	51° 12' 00" Lat - N
	120° 29' 00" Lon - W

Access/Parking

To reach the lake, take the Deadman-Vidette Road leading north from the Trans Canada Highway just west of the Deadman River Bridge. The road follows the Deadman River for what appears like an eternity until you pass by Mowich Lake, Skookum Lake and finally Deadman Lake. Vidette Lake is several kilometers north of Deadman Lake.

It is also possible to reach the lake from the Caribou Highway #97 by taking the Loon Lake Road to Vidette Lake. The main haul logging road leads northeast from Highway #97 south of Clinton. The paved portion of the road brings you past Loon Lake, a good gravel road (3400 Road) continues. At the 3437 km mark, take the right junction called the Clinton-Upper Loon Lake Road (3100 Rd). The Deadman-Vidette Road is the first major road heading south. That road will take you to the north end of Vidette Lake.

Other Options

If the fish are not biting at Vidette Lake, head south and try **Deadman, Snohoosh** or **Mowich Lakes**. For the backcountry hiker, there is a series of tiny mountain lakes to hike into. Bring a belly boat and plenty of fly patterns and you may be lucky enough to catch one of the rainbows that are said to reach 3 kg (8 lbs).

Lake Definition

Elevation:	762 m (2,500 ft)
Surface Area:	35 ha (86 ac)
Mean Depth:	14.3 m (46.8 ft)
Max Depth:	33 m (108 ft)
Perimeter:	6,885.5 m (22,590 ft)
Way Point:	51° 10' 00" Lat - N
	120° 54' 00" Lon - W

Fishing

The deep, 3 km long lake is truly the most picturesque of the lakes in the Deadman River Valley. It certainly isn't the best fishing lake in the area but it is worth a try.

In 1972, the lake was chemically treated to remove the course fish that were overrunning the lake. Unfortunately, the program was not entirely successful and so there are still plenty of sculpins in the lake. The recreation fishery is mainly comprised of small, wild rainbow in the 8-11 inch (20-27 cm) range but reports of fish to 0.45 kg (4 lbs) have been made. There are also some kokanee in the lake with some approaching 1 kg (3 lbs).

Vidette Lake is a fly fisherman's paradise as there are prolific hatches throughout the year. Leech, shrimp, damselfly nymph and dragonfly patterns all work depending on the hatch. The favorite flies for the lake are the Tom Thumb, Doc Spratley or Carey Special.

In the early spring, casting a fly towards shore is fairly productive. Towards the summer months, the rainbow retreat to the depths of the lake.

The kokanee are now reproducing naturally but there was a stocking of 10,000 fish in recent years to supplement a lull in the three year spawning cycle. By far the most effective way to fish the kokanee is to troll a Wedding Ring and worm or maggot. Dick Nites, tiny Spin-n-glows and Mepps spinners can meet with success as can casting a dry fly (the best one is a Grey Gnat). The kokanee tend to be small but you may be lucky enough to catch a fish in the 1 kg (2 lbs) range. The kokanee, in the summer months, stay near the surface of the lake contrary to the rainbow.

In the winter months, ice fishing is popular particularly with kokanee. Bait such as maggots, worms or corn on a hook and weight are productive.

Facilities

The Vidette Gold Mine Resort (1-800-700-3637) has been in operation since 1988 and offers year-round accommodation. The cabins have indoor plumbing, bedding & linen, kitchens and wood stoves. The resort has a wide array of services including a fly fishing school, canoes and rowboat rental, 6 camping sites, dining room, hot showers and guiding services.

For campers, the Vidette Lake Rec Site offers some rustic lakeshore camping at the south end of the lake.

Walloper Lake

Access/Parking

Walloper is found in the Lac Le Jeune area 36 km south of Kamloops. The lake is located just south of the Lac Le Jeune Exit (Exit 336) so the lake is easily accessed on a paved road.

Fishing

Walloper Lake is a perfect choice for a family outing. That is because the lake has many small rainbow trout that are willing to take just about anything offered. Also, the summer doldrums are not a problem at the lake so it is possible to have good success from early May after the ice is gone all the way to early November when the lake freezes over.

Walloper Lake is a tea-coloured lake, which is stocked with rainbow annually in the late 1980's. The lake has not been stocked since but the fish are spawning well. Also, an aerator has been installed to prevent winterkill.

Trolling a gang troll or a Flatfish is common practice. Green, yellow or black Flatfish all work.

For fly fishermen, sample the shoals and drop-offs with an attractor type fly pattern such as a Doc Spratley, Carey Special or Woolly Bugger.

Spincasters do well with a Flatfish, wedding ring, Deadly Dick or Panther Martin.

Facilities

There is a popular boat launch as well as a picnic area at the Walloper Provincial Park. The park is day-use only, but people do camp at the rustic trail access sites found near the boat launch. There is a resort on the south end of the lake. You can also camp at nearby Lac Le Jeune.

Other Options

Nearby **Lac Le Jeune** is one of the most popular destinations in the area. We highlight this lake on page 48 of this book.

Lake Definition

Elevation:	1,305 m (4,284 ft)
Surface Area:	42.6 ha (90 ac)
Mean Depth:	2.9 m (9.5 ft)
Max Depth:	7.8 m (25.6 ft)
Perimeter:	3,680 m (12,073 ft)
Way Point:	50° 29' 00" Lat - N
	120° 32' 00" Lon - W

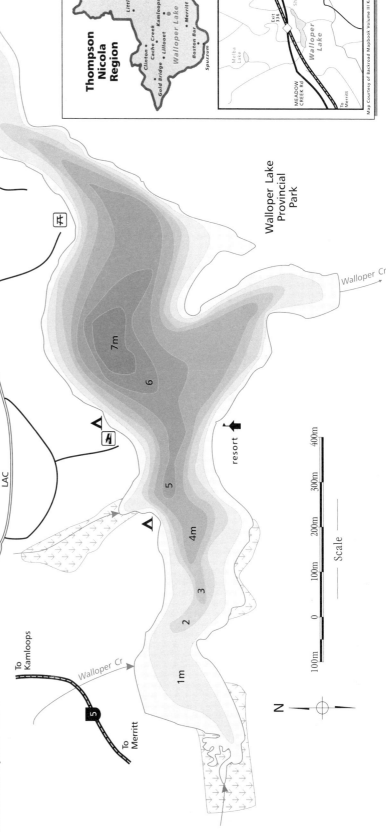

Thompson Nicola Region

Little Fort
Sicamous
Salmon Arm
Clinton
Cache Creek
Kamloops
Gold Bridge
Lillooet
Merritt
Boston Bar
Spuzzum

To Kamloops
Exit 336
Shambrook Lake
Lac Le Jeune
MEADOW CREEK Rd
Walloper Lake
To Merritt
Molba Lake
Walloper Lake

Map Courtesy of Backroad Mapbook Volume III Kamloops/Okanagan

ROAD

LE JEUNE

Walloper Lake Provincial Park

LAC

Walloper Lake Provincial Park

To Hwy 5
Exit 336

7m
6
5
4m
3
2
1m

resort

Walloper Cr

Walloper Cr

To Kamloops

To Merritt

N

100m 0 100m 200m 300m 400m
Scale

Young Lake

Access/Parking

Young Lake is found south of Green Lake in the lower Cariboo Region. To reach the lake, travel to 70 Mile House and take the North Bonaparte Road heading northeast. Continue to the Egan-Bonaparte Road heading southeast. That road is found east of TinCup Lake and after the North Bonaparte Road runs next to the Rayfield River. Follow the Egan-Bonaparte Road until you reach the Boule-Young Lake Road intersection. Hang a right on that road and follow the road to the west end of Young Lake.

Several other road systems access the lake but be careful as the bridges have been removed over the Bonaparte River to the west of Young Lake. We recommend having a good, up-to-date map when trying to access the lake.

Fishing

Young Lake has a very steep shoreline on the south end with rocky outcrops and bedrock extending down to the shoreline. The water drops off rapidly to a depth of 65 m.

Young Lake is generally a trolling lake with gang trolls and small lures being the gear of choice. The lake is fishable in early May until early November. The summer fishery remains active for rainbows that reach 1.5 kg (3-4 lbs) given the water is deep and does not warm significantly in the heat of the summer.

For fly fishermen, the late spring caddisfly hatch offers good dry fly fishing. Using a shrimp pattern on a sinking line is also very productive.

Small kokanee can be caught by trolling a Willow Leaf and worm at 3-6 m (10-20 ft) as slow as possible. A Dick Nite, pink Flatfish or small pink spin-n-glow are other options.

Facilities

Young Lake has a boat launch and camping area. There are also private cabins along the north shore of the lake.

Other Options

Moose Lake is found north of Young Lake but is known more for a nice camping area than a great fishing lake. As with most lakes in the area, the lake can produce small trout, especially in the summer and fall.

Lake Definition

Elevation:	936 m (3,070 ft)
Surface Area:	252 ha (622 ac)
Mean Depth:	20.3 m (94 ft)
Max Depth:	66 m (217 ft)
Perimeter:	24,800 m (81,344 ft)
Way Point:	51° 15' 00" Lat - N
	120° 58' 00" Lon - W

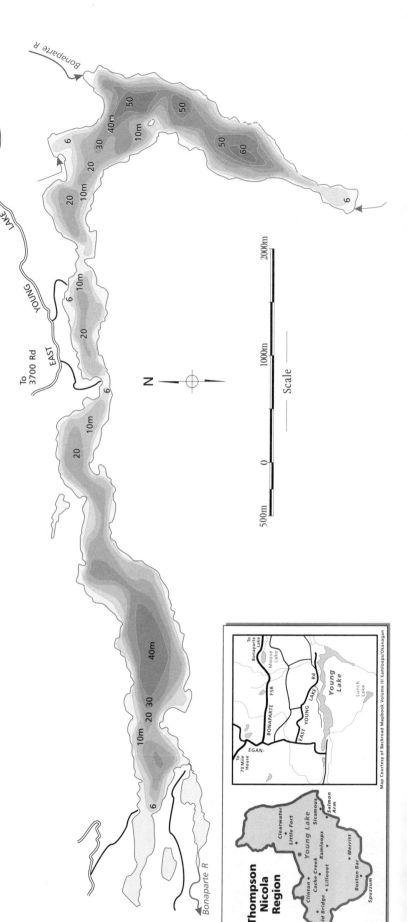

Map Courtesy of Backroad Mapbook Volume III Kamloops/Okanagan

IMPORTANT PHONE NUMBERS

Road & Trail Conditions

Clearwater Forest District 1-250-587-6700
Kamloops Forest District 1-250-371-6500
Highway Reports 1-800-663-4997
Lillooet Forest District 1-250-256-1200
Merritt Forest District 1-250-378-8400
Updates .... *www.backroadmapbooks.com*

Parks

B.C. Parks 1-250-387-4550
B.C. Parks (Kamloops) .... 1-250-851-3000, www.env.gov.bc.ca
Park Reservations 1-800-689-9025

Fish & Wildlife

Fish & Wildlife (Kamloops) 1-250-371-6200
Wilderness Watch 1-800-465-4336

Conservation Officers

Clearwater 1-250-674-3722
Clinton 1-250-459-2341
Kamloops 1-250-371-6200
Lillooet 1-250-256-4636
Merritt 1-250-378-8489

Resorts & Ranches

Ark Park Resort 1-250-573-3878
Bolean Lake Lodge 1-250-558-9008
Caverhill Resort 1-250-672-9806
Corbett Lake Country Inn 1-250-378-4334
Crystal Waters Guest Ranch 1-888-593-2252
Douglas Lake Ranch 1-800-663-4838
Dunn Lake Resort 1-250-674-2344
Hyas Lake Resort 1-250-319-1404
Heffley Lake Resort 1-250-578-7251
Knouff Lake Resort 1-888-562-0555
Johnson Lake Resort 1-250-828-6966
Lac Le Jeune Resort 1-800-561-5253
Lakeside Country Inn 1-800-909-7434
Logan Lake Lodge 1-250-523-9466
North Barriére Lake Resort 1-250-376-9922
Peter Hope Lodge 1-250-371-7330
Pinantan Lake Resort 1-250-573-3534
Roche Lake Resort 1-250-828-2007
Salmon Lake Resort 1-800-663-4838
Sky Blue Water Resort 1-250-256-7633
Thunderbird Lodge 1-250-371-9946
Tunkwa Lake Fishing Camp & Resort 1-250-523-9697
Vidette Gold Mine Resort 1-800-700-3637
Woody Life Village Resort 1-250-374-3833

...the start of every adventure!!

**Volume I:
Southwestern BC**

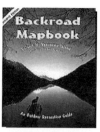
**Volume II:
Vancouver Island**

**Volume III:
Kamloops/Okanagan**

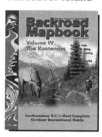
**Volume IV:
The Kootenays**

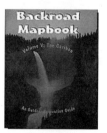
**Volume V:
The Cariboo**

**Volume VI:
Central BC**

To obtain your book for $15.95, see your local
outdoor retailer, bookstore or contact:

Backroad Mapbooks
232 Anthony Court
New Westminster, B.C.
V3L 5T5, Canada
P. (877) 520-5670 F. (604) 520-5630

orders@backroadmapbooks.com

www.backroadmapbooks.com

Published By:

**Fishing BC
Lower Mainland**

**Fishing BC
Thompson Nicola**

The Authors

Russell Mussio (left) graduated from the University of British Columbia with a
degree in Leisure and Sports Administration. He formed Mussio Ventures Ltd.
in 1993 with his brother, Wesley, in order to publish, distribute and market outdoor
recreation guidebooks and maps.

Wesley Mussio (right) is a Registered Professional Forester and a Lawyer practicing
as a trial lawyer with the law firm of Lindsay Kenney in Vancouver, BC.

Russell and Wesley are avid outdoorsmen. Whenever they are not researching
and writing a new book, they are enjoying the great outdoors.

Help Us Help You

A comprehensive resource such as *Fishing BC* could not be put together
without a great deal of help and support. Despite our best efforts to ensure
that everything is accurate, errors do occur. If you see any errors or omis-
sions, please continue to let us know.

Mail to:

Mussio Ventures Ltd.
232 Anthony Court
New Westminster, B.C. V3L 5T5

All updates will be posted on our web site:
www.backroadmapbooks.com

Phone: 1-877-520-5670
Fax: 1-604-520-5630
E-mail: updates@backroadmapbooks.com